Look Homeward, America

Look Homeward, America

In Search of Reactionary Radicals and Front-Porch Anarchists

Bill Kauffman

ISI BOOKS

2006

Kauffman, Bill, 1959–

Look homeward, America : in search of reactionary radicals and
front-porch anarchists / Bill Kauffman. — 1st ed. — Wilmington, DE : ISI
Books, 2006.

    p. ; cm.

    ISBN-13: 978-1-932236-87-3
    ISBN-10: 1-932236-87-2
    Includes bibliographical references and index.

    1. Radicalism—United States. 2. Right and left (Political science) 3.
Patriotism—United States. 4. United States—Politics and government—
2001–5. Political culture—United States. I. Title.

JK1764 .K38 2006
320.5/0973—dc22   0604

Published in the United States by:

    ISI Books
    Intercollegiate Studies Institute
    Post Office Box 4431
    Wilmington, DE 19807-0431

        Book design by Beer Editorial and Design

        Manufactured in the United States of America

for my teachers—
with gratitude, respect, and apologies where necessary

Contents

Acknowledgments

I met Jeremy Beer in Savannah, Georgia, at a Liberty Fund conference on "The Work of Wendell Berry." I liked him immediately, and not only for his agreeable surname. He is a credit to the Hoosier race and a delight to work with. Thanks, too, to Allan Carlson for organizing the conference and Liberty Fund for footing the liquor bill.

For assistance and encouragement in manifold ways I thank Jason Peters, Kirsten Manges, Jeff Nelson, Gore Vidal, Alan Crawford, Tim Rives, Jane Schmieder, the late Barber B. Conable Jr., Kathryn Hodson, Jesse Walker, Geoffrey Gneuhs, Kate Dalton Boyer, Sanford Church, Don Read, Peter H. Clune, and editors Karl Zinsmeister, Jeffrey St. Clair, Erich Eichman, Tom Fleming, Marty Zupan, Chilton Williamson, and Chris Check.

Finally, and from the beginning, Lucine and Gretel Kauffman remind me daily why a radical should also be a reactionary, why an anarchist needs a front porch, and why this American always looks homeward.

Introduction

*"Reaction is the most radical of programs; it aims at cutting
away the overgrowth and getting back to the roots."*
—ALLEN TATE

I am an American patriot. A Jeffersonian decentralist. A fanatical
localist. And I am an anarchist. Not a sallow garret-rat translating
Proudhon by pirated kilowatt, nor a militiaman catechized by the
Classic Comics version of *The Turner Diaries*; rather, I am the love child of
Henry Thoreau and Dorothy Day, conceived amidst the asters and gold-
enrod of an Upstate New York autumn.

Like so many of the subjects of this book, I am also a reactionary
radical, which is to say I believe in peace and justice but I do not believe in
smart bombs, daycare centers, Wal-Mart, television, or Melissa Etheridge's
test-tube baby.

"Reactionary radicals" are those Americans whose political radicalism (often inspired by the principles of 1776 and the culture of the early
America) is combined with—in fact, flows from—a deep-set social "conservatism."

These are not radicals who wish to raze venerable institutions and
make them anew: they are, in fact, at antipodes from the warhead-clutching
egghead described by (the reactionary radical) Robert Lee Frost:

> With him the love of country means
> Blowing it all to smithereens
> And having it all made over new

These reactionary radicals—a capacious category in which I include Dorothy Day, Carolyn Chute, Grant Wood, Eugene McCarthy, Wendell Berry, and a host of other cultural and political figures—have sought to tear down what is artificial, factitious, imposed by remote and often coercive forces and instead cultivate what is local, organic, natural, and family-centered.

In our almost useless political taxonomy, some are labeled "right wing" and others are tucked away on the left, but in fact they are kin: embodiments of an American cultural-political tendency that is wholesome, rooted, and based in love of family, community, local self-rule, and a respect for permanent truths. We find them not at the clichéd "bloody crossroads" but at thrillingly fruitful conjunctions: think Robert Nisbet by way of Christopher Lasch, or Russell Kirk by way of Paul Goodman. Think, always, of things tending homeward.

Not that I have never strayed from home. From Alaska to North Dakota, from visits with pacifist homesteaders to neo-Confederate painters, I have sought what is vital, alive, flavorful, and seditious in American political life. I started in the employ of Pat Moynihan, the most intellectually impressive liberal Democrat of postwar America, and have ended at a homespun anarchism deep-dyed in the native grain, as the sort of typewriter agrarian who, quite unsuspectingly, bakes zucchini bread with cucumbers, somewhat in the manner of blessed old Henry Thoreau taking his wash in from Walden Pond for mom to do on weekends.

My favorite America is the America of holy fools and backyard radicals, the America whose eccentric voice is seldom heard anymore in the land of Clear Channel, Disney, and Gannett. It is the America of third parties, of Greenbackers and Libertarians and village atheists and the "conservative Christian anarchist" party whose founder and only member was Henry Adams. It is the America that is always disappearing but whose rebirth is written in the face of every homeschooled girl, every poet of the wheat fields, every boy who chooses baseball over Microsoft, birdhouse-building over the U.S. Army. It is the America of those who harbor the crazy belief that Middle American culture might add up to something more than the oeuvre of Dean Jones.

Yet while I like a tidy Manichean division as much as the next zealot, I readily if glumly concede that as Middle Americans the fault lies in ourselves, as I learned on a sojourn in Columbus, Mississippi, a few years back. We drove into this lovely town of antebellum mansions and magnolia-fragrant avenues, stopping at a local eatery. I am a hopeful romantic and expected to find vatic old black men whittling on benches, laconic loafers drawling wittily on courthouse steps, and tomboyish Nelle Harper Lee hiding in the bushes, taking it all down. Eh, not quite, Bill. The first Columbian we encountered was a sullen youth from Teenage Central Casting, playing the usual corporate schlock on his boombox. We entered the diner and were seated behind four ladies with mellifluous Mississippi accents. They spent the next half-hour recounting the plot of the previous night's episode of *Friends*, that vulgar and witless NBC sitcom by which archeologists will someday condemn our civilization.

I wanted to confront them, plead with them: Look. Here you are, citizens of the economically poorest yet culturally richest state in the union, the state that gave us Eudora Welty, the Delta Blues, William Faulkner, Muddy Waters, Shelby Foote, and yet you not only consume but crave the packaged products of cocaine-addled East/West Coast greedheads who despise you as ignorant rednecks and stupid crackers. Get off your knees, Mississippi!

Well, I didn't say that, checked as I am by that Upstate New York reserve. But I meant every word I didn't say. Until Americans take the Chute route of rejecting the remote and pestilential institutions that mean us harm, and of choosing the free, the local, the life-givingly anarchic, the Columbuses will rot into Columbines.

I interlard my work with memoir and personal asides the way my wife adds garlic to her cooking: liberally, unabashedly, with the conviction that flavor and spice make savor and nice. But a little extra garlic never hurt anyone. Except the undead.

I begin *Look Homeward, America* with two Catholic Democrats, Senator Eugene McCarthy and my old boss, Senator Daniel Patrick Moynihan. McCarthy, whom I interviewed several times, was a constitutionalist liberal in an age of extraconstitutional liberalism. He was the link between the Old Progressives of the Upper Midwest—boreal Jeffersonians—and the ADA liberals; as time went by and his profile sharpened, McCarthy proved to be much closer to Bob LaFollette than to Adlai Stevenson.

Pat Moynihan's extraordinary career informed—gave shape to— many of the currents that have twisted and twined the Democratic Party and that, withal, drove me away from liberalism. He was both Cassandra and coward, tower and trimmer.

At his best, Moynihan was a blend of radical and reactionary, in the manner of the great postwar literary American patriots: Edmund Wilson, Gore Vidal, Norman Mailer, Dwight Macdonald, Paul Goodman. Like Eugene McCarthy, he was precocious in his critique of the devastating effect the Interstate Highway System would have on American life. He descried (and decried), with considerable foresight, the virtual expulsion of devout Catholic Democrats from the party, and the ways that this purge would deprive the Democrats of their anchorage in the neighborhood. He was also a late-blooming skeptic of American Empire, as his fulsome eulogists conveniently ignored.

In between . . . well, he sure got good press. But more on that later.

Oh, Pat, I hardly knew ye, yet I sure as hell knew I didn't want to be like ye. Disgusted by the timidity and lack of imagination of liberal Democrats, afire with belief in absolute liberty, I crossed the grand ballroom of American politics. . . . No, that's not right. Better to say that I left the palace and followed the din to the tarpaper shack way down by the laissez river. I jumped into libertarianism as an editor of *Reason*, the oldest and largest of libertarian magazines and a harbinger of the market-worship that would overtake—that would briefly invigorate, but then deaden—late-twentieth-century America.

If only the libertarians simply sought maximum personal freedom: legalized dope and criminalized taxation. Neat inversions, those. And clearly part of the zeitgeist, to swipe a favorite term of the movement. Alas, the movement, and *Reason* in particular, had been infected at birth by the misanthropic pulp-novelist Ayn Rand, who hissed at William F. Buckley Jr., "Mr. Buckley, you are too intelligent to be-leef in gott." The priestess Rand's only god was selfishness, which she deemed a "virtue" in the title of one of her unreadable nonfiction word-clots.

My casual confession—exaggeration, really—that I was "a good Catholic boy" earned me the enmity of a Randian founder of the magazine, one of those English-as-a-fourth-language Eastern European immigrants who had forsaken his homeland only to seek to bring the spirit of Soviet bloc regimentation to our country, à la Dr. Strangelove, Edward Teller, who was always pestering idiosyncratic Americans to take up the grey, dreary, antihuman metric system. Anyway, our libertarian immigrant asked with (Joe, not Gene) McCarthyite urgency in one confidential missive, "Do you notice whether Kauffman interjects his theistic, altruistic ethical and political views into his editorial decisions and opinions?"

Well, uh, yes, I suppose I did, but I would also, by the grace of that Gott who conjoins congenial subeditors, meet a dazzling array of kooks and patriots, of Mormon polygamists and bellicose economists and would-be Pizarros who plotted to colonize Titan, the largest moon of Saturn, as an outpost of extraterrestrial libertarianism.

I cannot think of the libertarians without laughing, and yet, on the great issue of the day, they were dead right. They diagnosed the twentieth century's homicidal malady: the all-powerful state, which in the name of the workers of the world, the master race, and even making the world safe for democracy had slaughtered tens, nay hundreds, of millions of human beings whose misfortune it had been to run afoul of ideologues wielding state power.

I next fell into queer company with the "paleoconservatives," that intoxicating (and often intoxicated) mishmash of libertarians, traditionalist conservatives, and reactionary hippies whose flagship magazine, *Chronicles*, became, for perhaps a lustrum, the most galvanizing, infuriating, brilliantly written political journal in America. For a moment, the old boundaries seemed to have fallen away; bizarrely apt alliances formed: Jewish Confederates, Latin Mass Catholics, Ed Abbeyesque tree-hugging beer-can throwers, radical businessmen who admired Jerry Brown, and gay Quakers who campaigned for Pat Buchanan. Mix it all together and you get Ross Perot. To whom—despite . . . you know—I will ever tip my cap.

The paleos excited more lurid portraits and sputtering denunciations than any political movement since the New Left. As a sojourner on their left fringe, I agreed with certain of the criticisms while bemoaning the modern practice of demonizing all dissenters as furtively creepy thought criminals. For what a glorious hodgepodge these people were! The guru of the libertarian paleos, the combative economist and joyful iconoclast Murray Rothbard, was a gnomic 5'3" nonbelieving Jew who adored cathedrals; championed the Black Panthers while also boasting that he had been founder, president, and pretty much the only member of Columbia University Students for Strom Thurmond in the 1948 presidential election; and once woke his wife JoAnn out of a sound sleep to declare, in his gleeful squawk, "That bastard Eli Whitney *didn't* invent the cotton gin!"

The paleos ranged all over the political lot, from Port Huron New Leftists to John Birchers, and American politics staggered from the shock when a former Nixon polemicist and fierce Cold Warrior, Pat Buchanan, adopted isolationist paleo themes in his presidential campaigns and shocked the GOP in that redoubt of flintiness, New Hampshire.

It couldn't last. The paleos dissolved—or rather, they erupted—in bile and drunken haymakers. Yet the anti-globalist, Little American tendency to which they gave voice and shape is likely to grow (perhaps even burgeon) as the most intellectually rigorous and sentimentally appealing electoral alternative to our two-for-the-price-of-one parties. At its best, it embraces the gentle, amusedly tolerant and neighborly anarchism that makes small-town America so sweet.

My wanderings had taken me from the populist flank of liberalism to the agrarian wing of Don't Tread on Me libertarianism to the peace-and-love left wing of paleoconservatism, which is to say that I had been always on the outside—an outsider even among outsiders—attracted to the spirit of these movements but never really comfortable within them, never willing even to call myself by their names. When asked, I was simply an Independent. A Jeffersonian. An anarchist. A (cheerful!) enemy of the state, a reactionary Friend of the Library, a peace-loving football fan. And here, as Gerry and the Pacemakers once sang, is where I'll stay.

Look Homeward, America—and yes, the echoes of Thomas Wolfe and George McGovern are intentional—offers an alternative to the American Empire whose subject no true-hearted American would wish to be. Mine is a Middle American, profoundly un-imperial patriotism based in love of American music, poetry, places, quirks and commonalities, historical crotchets, holy fools and eminent Kansans. It is *not* the sham patriotism of the couch-sitter who sings "God Bless America" as the bombs light up his television, or the chickenhawk who loves little of his country beyond its military might.

I celebrate, I affirm old-fashioned refractory Americanism, the home-loving rebel spirit that inspires anarchists and reactionaries to save chestnut trees from the highway-wideners and rural schools from the monstrous maw of the consolidators, and leads along the irenic path of a fresh-air patriotism whose opposition to war and empire is based in simple love of country.

Yes, I know, "we can't turn back the clock." (But did you ever wonder if perhaps your watch tells the wrong time?) This is America, land of progress: we can't go backward! God how I know it. For I have sat in darkening mizzly forenight sipping pale ale in Springfield, Illinois's hipster-Mexican restaurant reading Vachel Lindsay poetize "the City of my Discontent" as the jukebox plays "Don't You Want Me, Baby?" and gazed out the window at the mottled concrete moonscape of the land where Lincoln walked at midnight.

Springfield was urban-renewed into Gehenna. Sherman's bummers couldn't have done it any better. But the faith demonstrated by poor mad Vachel endures. Hell, it animates me.

Now, I do not claim to be the archetypal American. If my ethnic mix is typically mongrel, stretching from Italy to Ireland, so are my politics a blend of Catholic Worker, Old Right libertarian, Yorker transcendentalist, and delirious localist. So my story is singular but also strangely representative. We live in an age in which Americans by the millions have lost faith in a system that seems, at best, alien, and at worst, repressive. I, too, started in the mainstream, but I found it placidly sinister, so I took a trip down the tributaries, left and right and great plunging cataracts, till I found that my faith in the oldest, simplest, most radical America had been renewed.

Robert Frost put his faith in the "insubordinate Americans," throaty dissenters and ornery traditionalists, and this book is for and about them—those Americans who reject Empire; who cherish the better America, the *real* America; who cannot be broken by the Department of Homeland Security, who will not submit to the PATRIOT Act, and who will make the land acrid and bright with the stench and flame of burnt national ID cards when we—should we—cross that Orwellian pass. This is still our country, you know. Don't let Big Brother and the imperialists take it from us.

CHAPTER ONE

Two Independent Catholic Liberals Diverged in a Wood

Eugene McCarthy and Pat Moynihan

"The effect of power and publicity on all men is the aggravation of self, a sort of tumor that ends by killing the victim's sympathies."

—HENRY ADAMS

In March 1968, Eugene McCarthy earned the everlasting gratitude of American patriots when he came within a beagle's ear of defeating Lyndon B. Johnson in the New Hampshire primary, thus forcing into retirement one of the more repulsive monograms ever to occupy the presidency. His 1968 campaign—an act of political suicide—gave voice to an incipient antiwar tendency in what had been an extremely hawkish Democratic Party. (Bob Dole's crack about the "Democrat wars" of the twentieth century had been true enough to earn him his fifteen minutes on the cross.) McCarthy's strong showing in the New Hampshire primary drove LBJ back to his ranch, Bobby Kennedy into the race, and McCarthy into a kind of involuntary exile from which he never really emerged.

"I haven't been asked to speak to Democrats since 1967," he said to me and anyone else who ever interviewed him, a pinch of asperity dotting his matter-of-fact shrug. Independence has its rewards, but the party, as the renegade soon learns, is over.

Until his death in December 2005, Senator Eugene McCarthy was

America's senior statesman without a party. Not that the Democrats deserved him, or even knew what to make of him: McCarthy's contention that we are becoming a country in which "everyone belongs to a corporation and everyone else belongs to the federal government" made him unwelcome in a party that regards Bill Bradley as a cerebral maverick.

My first interview with Gene McCarthy took place in September 1986 in a Washington office supplied him by Harcourt Brace, his publisher; the resulting profile was spiked for ideological reasons too dreary to relate. Suffice to say that think tanks are aptly named: they are tanks whose guns and treads are aimed at thought.

Ten years later, in January 1996, we chatted in McCarthy's hotel room at the Algonquin, which required me to overcome my pathological aversion to the Vampire City, though just barely: I rode the Hound into the Port Authority (a ten-hour trip), sucked in the fetid air of Times Square upon debarking, hoofed it to the Algonquin, where I stupidly forgot to take a peek at the round table, and after a pleasant ninety minutes disappeared into the Port Authority for my bumpy hegira.

Our talk appeared in *Chronicles* and later as a chapter in McCarthy's *No-Fault Politics*, compiled for Times Books by Keith Burris, a Manchester, Connecticut, newspaper editorialist. Funny thing, though: passages from our chat in which McCarthy discoursed on immigration, about which he had become decidedly unenthusiastic, and on the influence of ethnic or religious lobbies on U.S. foreign policy disappeared into the Times Books memory hole. McCarthy's laments over bilingual education, Rupert Murdoch's communications octopus, and the Cuban and Israel lobbies vanished into that vast pit of liberal censorship known as "Discretion." The better part of valor, perhaps, but the bigger part of cowardice.

And Gene McCarthy, whatever his peccadilloes, was never a coward.

Had he played by Their rules, Eugene McCarthy at twilight would have been an eminence grise, a grey Clark Clifford with a rotted soul, instead of the persona non grata he became.

His senectitude did not, to put it mildly, bring him honors. For in his eighty-ninth year, McCarthy was broadsided by a thirty-year-old Brit biographer named Dominic Sandbrook.

You know you're not in for a Doris Kearns Goodwin/David McCullough hagiography when your chronicler uses as an epigraph a character assessment by the thuggish Robert Kennedy. ("Gene just isn't a nice person," sneered RFK. And isn't the three-letter monogram usually a tipoff to a sinister force?)

"For his youthful volunteers, McCarthy was a brave and dashing champion who would unseat the brutal Johnson and bring a swift and just end to the carnage of the Vietnam War," writes Sandbrook, who is eager to show us just how wrong they were. His McCarthy is a "frivolous maverick" whose frivolity consisted of such ridiculous acts as writing poetry and calling for the legalization of marijuana, and whose maverickness manifested itself in lese majeste remarks directed at such worthies as Walter Mondale, LBJ ("a barbarian"), and, most damningly, John F. Kennedy ("shallow, unintelligent, and unequipped for high office, his reputation bloated with his father's money," in Sandbrook's paraphrase).

Would that American politics were filled with such frivolous mavericks.

Born in 1916, Eugene McCarthy enjoyed a happy, baseball-playing childhood in the small German-Irish Catholic town of Watkins, Minnesota. He studied with the Benedictine monks at nearby St. John's University; his formative years were deeply Catholic, a Minnesotan mix of reactionary and radical.

At St. John's, where McCarthy later taught, the air was fresh with the influence of the saintly Dorothy Day and her Catholic Worker movement, which gently preached a cooperativist anarchism. He met Day and the holy fool Peter Maurin and ever after spoke warmly of "distributive justice" as opposed to "equality" and "fairness," which, he said, have "neither historical nor philosophical bearing." The bright, acerbic McCarthy was much taken with his church's rural life initiatives, which encouraged small-scale farming, home production, and the village economy. In best Midwestern fashion, McCarthy was also an isolationist pacifist before Pearl Harbor.

McCarthy read Chesterton, Belloc, and the Catholic Distributists who were seeking humane and decentralist alternatives to communism, fascism, and corporate capitalism. He bought eighty acres of land from his dad and planned a cooperative farming community. Alas, Gene and his wife Abigail turned out to be theoretical agrarians who would rather read about the land than labor in it, and in a not so simple twist of fate, he fell into politics.

McCarthy's mentor, Father Virgil Michel, called communism "an all-devouring, godless collectivism . . . certain to crush all human and spiritual values." Father Michel was right on the money, of course. But where the good monk would combat communism in the Catholic Worker way, through the establishment of human-scale institutions compatible with a Christian anarchism, young Gene McCarthy joined the social democrat Hubert Humphrey in purging Minnesota's Democratic-Farmer-Labor Party of its Henry Wallace lefties, narrowing "the permissible range of political debate within Minnesota," as one historian has noted, and making the Upper Midwest safe for Harry Truman.

Given that Nagasaki Harry ranks right down there with Woodrow Wilson and LBJ as a presidential enemy of liberty, one wonders: Would we really have been worse off had the muddleheaded Henry Wallace Democrats not been hunted down like rats by the welfare-warfare liberals of Americans for Democratic Action?

In any event, McCarthy was elected to Congress from St. Paul in 1948: news of his victory came by phone as he and his supporters were saying the rosary. He ran as a "quintessential Fair Deal liberal" and his subsequent record was every bit as drab as one would expect. If it cost money, McCarthy voted for it, without fail, down the line; from 1949 to 1958, he voted "right" on all fifty-six of the AFL-CIO's "key votes."

In foreign affairs, he traded the grand Shipstead-Lindbergh isolationist tradition of Minnesota for Humphrey interventionism, scolding Taft conservatives for their "failure to recognize the basic evil of communism." McCarthy even spoke in favor of HHH's 1954 bill to ban the Communist Party.

So while he was critical of the other McCarthy, Wisconsin's Tail Gunner Joe, Minnesota's Gene never really cast a comminatory net over that mope's parade of grim communists, squirrely snitches, and alcoholic apostates who gave such a caliginous cast to the Senate hearing rooms of the early 1950s. What energy was wasted in promoting and combatting an alien ideology that never had a snowball's chance in Las Vegas of taking root in American soil! Television, highways, and suburbanization were changing America in the most profound ways, but the red-hunters and the reds, locked in their death embrace, never even noticed. (So what, you ask, should the civil libertarian do about communists in government jobs? "Abolish the jobs," replied the anarchist Frank Chodorov. But who listens to anarchists?)

McCarthy's personal style was cool, detached, ironic: one almost expects to find photos of him shooting heroin with Johnny Depp. He was a loner, a cynical wit, handsome star of the House Democratic baseball team, and chronic skipper of the tedious meetings of the Post Office Committee.

Elected to the Senate in 1958, McCarthy "struck observers as listless and lazy," according to *New Republic* columnist Richard Stout, whose prose struck observers with the force of twenty Valium. McCarthy also despised the Kennedys. His contempt is usually ascribed to jealousy, but many of his coreligionists shared McCarthy's belief that the first Catholic president should not be a priapic skirt-chasing male bimbo.

We may look at McCarthy's first twenty years in politics and seek in vain for any evidence of the magnificently inspiring Catholic anarchism of his youth. By 1960, he was writing that "[g]overnment has a positive and natural function to assist man in the pursuit of perfection and happiness," an idea at odds with the Catholic Worker and in fact the writing on the road signs to school busing, urban renewal, and the progressive programs that destroyed much of American community life in the Vital Center years.

As a party-line Democrat, McCarthy's only criticism of internationalist Republicans was that they didn't spend enough on foreign aid. Like JFK, he slammed President Eisenhower for penny-pinching on the military-industrial complex. "Nowhere did he contemplate the limits of American power or the morality of intervention overseas," writes biographer Sandbrook.

Then came Vietnam, and with it the salutary influence of the courageous Arkansas Democratic Senator William Fulbright, a kind of Tory Confederate anti-imperialist whose chairmanship of the Foreign Relations Committee did so much to smash the suffocating consensus of the early 1960s.

Vietnam changed McCarthy, drew him back, at least partway, to his St. John's roots. In 1964 he was an unquestioning supporter of the Gulf of Tonkin Resolution; by 1967, in *The Limits of Power,* he was saying that "America's contribution to world civilization must be more than a continuous performance demonstration that we can police the planet." Tentatively, then with gusto, he began uttering "the first criticism of the Cold War orthodoxy by a major candidate in a presidential campaign since 1948." Since, that is, Henry Wallace.

When Undersecretary of State Nicholas Katzenbach haughtily informed Fulbright's committee that a presidential declaration of war was "outmoded in the international arena," McCarthy walked out of the room and told a reporter, "Someone's got to take them on. And if I have to run for president to do it, I'm going to do it."

One of the monks at St. John's told McCarthy in late '67, "*Viriliter agite*"—Act manfully. He did. And in so doing he gave antiwar patriots who believed in the two-party system a meaningful choice in 1968. (In retrospect, '68 was the Year of the Gopher, as the most prominent antiwar figures in politics and music were a pair of Minnesota poets, Eugene McCarthy and the Iron Range's Bob Dylan. The latter, who was sagely advising young Americans, "Don't follow leaders," would write in the liner notes to his 1993 album *World Gone Wrong*, "give me a thousand acres of tractable land & all the gang members that exist & you'll see the Authentic alternative lifestyle, the Agrarian one.")

"They say I'm committing political suicide," said McCarthy as he launched his campaign. "Well, I'd rather do that and face up to the wrongness of the war than die of political old age."

The Johnson forces redbaited: "The Communists in Vietnam are watching the New Hampshire primary," warned the president's radio ads. "They are hoping for a divided America. Don't vote for . . . surrendering. Support our fighting men." (That Americans might best "support our troops" by reuniting them with their families seems never to occur to those who would choke the country with their yellow ribbons.)

He sounded unlike anyone else in American politics. Whilst Americans were benumbed by the platitudes and programs of Humphrey, Muskie, Nixon, and Rockefeller, Eugene McCarthy was telling an audience, "America stands today at a critical point of decision: it can go in the direction of continued war and violence and further bureaucratization and automation of man, or it can go in the direction of personalism and reason and spiritual renewal." (Okay, so we took the wrong path.) The Catholic Worker echoes were audible, as they would be eight years later, sotto voce, in the Democratic primary campaign of America First cofounder and Dorothy Day admirer—and Kennedy in-law—Sargent Shriver.

In contrast to Bobby Kennedy's tepid dissent from the war his brother started, McCarthy struck at the root, telling a Portland, Oregon, rally that "involvement in Vietnam was no accident." Rather, it grew from "the idea that somehow we had a great moral mission to control the entire world." He called his campaign a "challenge to the militarization of American life and American foreign policy."

McCarthy raised a pile of Wall Street money from antiwar businessmen, which is perhaps why he later opposed campaign-finance reform so strenuously. The press claimed that hippies were forsaking hirsuteness by the communeful and going "Clean for Gene," but most of his young supporters were student council president–types, earnest liberals who preferred "Feelin' Groovy" to "Surrealistic Pillow."

On March 12, 1968, McCarthy polled 42.4 percent of the vote in the New Hampshire primary, coming within 230 votes of LBJ if one includes Republican write-ins. Four days later, the pavid Bobby Kennedy entered the race. At month's end, the homicidal Texan in the White House announced that he would not be a candidate for reelection.

Sam Houston Johnson, LBJ's brother, drawled, "There's something sort of stuck up about Gene. You get the impression that he's got a special pipeline to God and that they talk only Latin to each other." A good line, admittedly. McCarthy's medium-cool personality—horse-race journalist Jules Witcover called his "a sometimes lackadaisical, sometimes mystical, nearly always aloof manner"—was hardly the sort to produce bonhomie on the hustings. How many professional politicos would confess, immediately after toppling a president, that "boredom did have something to do with" his decision to run?

For a candidate said to be all wormwood and verjuice, McCarthy displayed a singular sense of humor. When asked his position on birth control as an element of foreign aid, he replied, "I am in favor of IUDs for sacred cows in India." But that was before flippancy was forbidden in the land of the free and the home of mandatory tolerance classes. (The wit remained, sardonic till the end. After Sandbrook's snide biography appeared, McCarthy wrote me, "One of the women who gave Dominic an interview said that Dom smelled bad. I told her that it was the usual odor of an Englishman of letters.")

McCarthy was a charmingly diffident candidate. Asked by Johnny Carson if he would be a good president, he replied, "I think I would be adequate." Horrors: self-deprecation! What will the World Community think? He also once "kept the *New York Times* columnist James Reston waiting while he composed a poem about wolverines." Well, what man born with a living soul *wouldn't* do that?

McCarthy cancelled dawn handshaking sessions at factory gates because "I'm not really a morning person." He preferred the company of poet Robert Lowell to that of the usual officious aides. Asked in 1968 for his greatest political influence—any Democrat with an ounce of insincerity would have said FDR or JFK—McCarthy cited Edmund Burke, and in the Burkean idea of "little platoons" we can see an alternative to the folding, bending, spindling, mutilating ideology of the Johnson-Humphrey Democrats.

Norman Mailer, as usual, hit McCarthy's nail on the head: "He was probably, left to his own inclinations, the most serious conservative to run for nomination since Robert Taft." It is a measure of the nescience and poltroonery of the modern American Right that only the left-wing conservatives, the Dwight Macdonalds and Mailers, appreciated McCarthy; the con-men of the organized Right were hustling for jobs in the Nixon campaign. Indeed, Richard Rovere fretted that McCarthy was too far left on foreign policy and too far right on domestic affairs to win a Democratic nomination.

McCarthy may be the best exemplar of the "left conservative" tendency that Mailer has explicated with such extraordinary trenchancy and to such overwhelming public indifference. As the pugilist of Brooklyn Heights told an interviewer in Scotland who asked "[W]hat's a left conservative?":

> . . . when you come to Edinburgh it's a remarkable city because it's the only city I know that gives me a sense of the past. In Europe right now it's sad—all the others including London you can see what modern high-rise architecture has done to absolutely destroy a sense of the past. So in that sense, I'm very much a conservative. I think

that if we lose a sense of the past, we've lost much more than we can ever calculate.

Most conservatives, if they're any good at all, but most of them are dreadful, are essentially instinctive. They feel "there's something about that tree that's more magnificent than anything I can name." When it comes to defending that tree against some highway that's going through, they usually give way to the highway because finally their friends come up to them who are also conservatives and say, "Listen, don't get in the way of that highway; it means a lot of money to a lot of people."

McCarthy, like his conservative admirer Russell Kirk, knew that the tree was magnificent. He even tried to describe it, with fitful success, in verse. ("Beech trees are ghostly but truthful./ Their bark will tell/ Who loved whom for years.") If he couldn't quite figure out how to save that tree from within the halls of Congress or on the series of airport tarmacs and robotized television appearances that constitute a presidential campaign, well, who could?

McCarthy's conception of the presidency was constitutional. He believed in a one-term "depersonalized" presidency; the biggest problem in government, he said, was "the concentration of power in the executive." He once said that two hours a day should be sufficient for a president to do all his necessary work, and he wasn't kidding.

The late political scientist James David Barber devised an infamous schematic by which he claimed we could determine the character of a *presidency* by the character of the *president*. Barber's—well, rebarbative—matrix depended upon two questions:

—"How much energy does the man invest in his presidency?" (Active-passive)

—"What is his general disposition and attitude toward wielding power?" (Positive-negative)

Barber was a liberal Democrat. Thus the taxonomically felicitous quadrant of active-positive is crammed with optimistic statist Democrats: FDR, Truman, Kennedy. McCarthy, by contrast, was a passive-negative, shunted to a lonely cell with dour Cal Coolidge as bunkmate. (The candidate anticipated Barber's pigeonhole with his campaign admission, "I think a little passivity in that office is all right.")

From our vantage point worlds away, McCarthy was always being cudgeled for his virtues. After the '68 campaign, a Houston McCarthyite confessed to second thoughts: "He was cold, imperious; I would have been afraid of him as president, for I fear he . . . may have been a do-nothing Ike type."

He scorned the strange notion of the presidency as a "bully pulpit" from which to sound off about dirty movies, national malaise, steroid use in baseball, and other matters far outside the constitutional purview of the executive. "Nixon said, 'I'm the moral leader of the country,'" observed McCarthy in one of our interviews. "Well, who the hell said . . . the President was supposed to be the moral leader?"

What followed was McCarthy at his best:

> ME: So if you had been elected in 1968, you wouldn't have used your office to campaign against free verse?

> McCARTHY: No, I'd concentrate on the real range of presidential responsibility. When Arthur Schlesinger defected to Bobby Kennedy from my campaign, he said I didn't have a conception of the strong presidency. He said I'd have been a president like Buchanan. That was a hell of a thing to say, because nobody knows what Buchanan was like. If he'd said I'd be like Grant, why, it means I'd have

been a drunk, but you say Buchanan and everybody imagines the worst. Four or five years later Schlesinger wrote the book on the imperial presidency. Poor Arthur: he's got energy; he never quits.

When Arthur defected, I said his defection is like a mistletoe blowing out of a beech tree in a slight wind. Some reporter said mistletoe is a parasite, isn't it? Well, I said, I hadn't really thought of that, but it's one of the worst parasites. So the guy wrote that I had called Arthur the ultimate parasite!

Arthur is the compleat historian: he wrote the Age of Jackson after it was over; he wrote the Age of Roosevelt while it was in progress; and he wrote the Age of Kennedy in advance.

Touché! (Arthur is nothing if not sensitive to the vagrant winds of fashion. In reviewing my cultural history of American isolationism, *America First!*, he volunteered that he had been maligned as an isolationist in the 1950s, a case of mistaken identity akin to confusing Aleister Crowley with Simone Weil.)

I do not want to misrepresent the McCarthy of '68 as some sort of quasi-libertarian Democrat. He betrayed his rural roots and demanded massive government spending on cities. In contrast to Bobby Kennedy's occasional concern for neighborhood integrity, McCarthy urged the central state to uproot "large numbers of Negro workers and their families to jobs and housing opportunities in the nation's suburbs," a piece of social engineering that would reduce human beings to the status of chessboard pawns, significant only in that they are black or white.

Yet he also scorned the "bureaucratic control" that "deprives the individual of all sense of individual initiative, and nourishes the belief that he can do nothing if it is not planned and organized and somehow fitted into a pattern of action."

He later rued the Minnesota Farmer-Labor Party's acceptance of the Great Society, "which was really quite foreign to the tradition of the Non-Partisan League and the Farmer-Laborites," as he told me. Whereas the New Deal, in McCarthy's analysis, sought "to change the structure and let welfare disappear because people didn't need it," LBJ's vision of social welfare "was we're going to have more Food Stamps and more help for the poor and more rent subsidies and more Medicaid." He retained a skepticism of social welfare programs, once remarking of the Great Society: "The general thrust of that program was to make ignorance, mental retardation, ill health, and even ugliness illegal."

When McCarthy left the Senate in 1970, one supporter fumed, "I cannot understand how he could abandon a useful career to indulge himself in a fancied talent for poetry." Tell such a fellow that making poetry is a far more beautiful and also more useful endeavor than making laws and he'll look at you the way George W. Bush might look at a page of Faulkner: with dull incomprehension mixed with a subsurface fury.

McCarthy never again came close to the Rose Garden (which he promised to replace with "humble vegetables" since "[y]ou'd have trouble announcing war in a cabbage patch"). He ran halfheartedly for the Democratic nomination in 1972 and then set up the Committee for a Constitutional Presidency—great name—that metamorphosed into his independent campaign of 1976, which gave birth to at least one aperçu: "It's not the fat [in the defense budget] that worries me. It's the lean that's causing all the trouble."

McCarthy never fell for the More Abundant Future patent medicine. During Watergate he cracked, "From 1789 to 1972, roughly, we went from Washington to Nixon, from John Adams to Spiro Agnew, from Alexander Hamilton to John Connally, from John Jay to John Mitchell. . . . You have to begin to wonder how much of that kind of progress you can stand."

In retirement, McCarthy wrote a book (*The Ultimate Tyranny*) warning of the accretion of power by alphabet-soup agencies, particularly the Internal Revenue Service. Like Edmund Wilson and Gore Vidal, he viewed the tax collectoriat as a lawless and arbitrary bureaucracy that feeds tyranny. McCarthy told me that "even the withholding of income tax was a bad idea. It made it easy for the government to collect and tended to have people be indifferent to their tax because they never got the money anyway. It raises a lot of questions about property and expropriation and eminent domain. . . . Liberals ought to be concerned, but . . ."

Yes, but. There's always that but.

McCarthy insisted that "the worst thing [Nixon] did was not Watergate, it was the enemies list. To use the power of the FBI and IRS to persecute people, to 'teach them a lesson,' was essentially fascist."

With "mischievous glee," McCarthy endorsed Reagan in 1980. The Democrats, he said, had become "the party of little other than the Department of Health, Education, and Welfare."

From his stone farmhouse at the foot of the Blue Ridge Mountains, he ran whimsical campaigns in 1988 and 1992, confirming the conventional view that "he was an unruly, disloyal eccentric who had squandered his own reputation in a series of self-indulgent campaigns that never ended in victory and had little impact on American politics and society."

That describes another quadrennial candidate from Minnesota, the silly internationalist Republican Harold Stassen, but not Eugene McCarthy. My God, McCarthy slayed LBJ, for which he still deserves the thanks of any American this side of Jack Valenti. And in later years he proposed solutions—some creative, others eccentric, the best rooted in his radical reactionary Catholic youth—to the maldistribution of wealth and power in these United States.

He proposed, for example, to increase the number of congressional districts to 2,000 and revitalize the electoral college by turning it into a deliberative convention of 2,500 members elected in districts of 100,000 people. "I'm pretty skeptical of every amendment adopted after the anti-slavery amendments," McCarthy told me in a remark so reactionary as to utterly disqualify him from participation in the parties of Hillary Clinton and Rudy Giuliani.

McCarthy was the only poet in the post-republic Senate. (I exempt the Maine Republican William Cohen, once celebrated as the "Rod McKuen of the Senate" even though Cohen never wrote a piece half as affecting as "Seasons in the Sun.") He was alert to the manipulation of language by the state, telling me:

> You could see the military-industrial complex developing . . . in the 1947 Defense Reorganization Act, and in the changing of the "War Department" into the "Department of Defense." I called the Pentagon and asked, how did this happen? There must have been a meeting where somebody said look, we're gonna change the name of this damn thing, because if we call it the War Department people are gonna say, "Where's the war? And if there isn't one, where are you gonna have it?" And we don't want to answer that question. So let's call it the Department of Defense because defense is unlimited. And it's true: we never declare war anymore. We just declare national defense.

Today that department is charged with the defense of the "homeland," a Nazi-Soviet term never used to denote the United States prior to the Age of Bush. Perhaps the most illuminating if unpublicized remark of any recent politico was the statement by Congressman Dan Burton (R-IN), chairman of the Government Reform Committee, who called the Department of Homeland Security "a Defense Department for the United States, if you will."

Meaning that the Department of Defense is a defense department for . . . ?

Eugene McCarthy was a constitutional liberal shaped by the isolationist Upper Midwest and Catholic social thought, and boy, doesn't that port look mighty attractive in the current storm?

"There is not always honor in failure," concludes McCarthy's hitman-biographer Sandbrook. Gene McCarthy, we are to believe, was a dishonorable failure, an arrogant, jealous, spiteful man who ought to have played the good soldier. He should have been a "professional, respectable and dedicated Democratic politician" who supported JFK, HHH, Muskie, Mondale, and the rest of his era's Democratic colossi. That he went into opposition—that, motivated by his Catholic conscience and his region's glorious radical lineage, he finally came to understand that the American Empire is the enemy of the American people—damns him in the court histories.

Well, to hell with them. Eugene McCarthy stood up against the machine; he walked out of the party; like the noble Senator Fulbright, he took his stand for the republic. Whatever his personal crotchets, he was an American patriot. And in case you haven't noticed, they are in damned short supply in Washington, D.C., these days.

I am a sucker for third parties, quixotic crusades, border bandits, charlatans, and raggedy-ass preachers on the political fringe. I remember sitting in the State College, Pennsylvania, airport talking cowboy-and-Indian movies with Russell Means, American Indian Movement founder, Wounded Knee upriser, and aspirant for the Libertarian Party presidential nomination, after we had spoken to the state's Libertarian Party convention in April 1987. "What's your favorite?" I asked Means, and in his most solemn Grave Red Man countenance, with a far-off gaze bespeaking smallpox-infected blankets and Trails of Tears now covered with two-acre-minimum lot developments, he whispered, half-conspiratorially, "You know what the best one is? The best movie ever?" No, I shook my head. Tell me. Tell me, oh wise one. "*Mandingo*," he intoned. A Ken Norton vehicle, for Chrissakes, a swelteringly lurid fleshpot of miscegenation! It's as if I walked in on Aleksandr Solzhenitsyn when he was hidden away in Vermont, his trappings all monkish and cloistered, and found him sprawled on the Naugahyde couch watching *The Pom-Pom Girls*.

Means lost in his bid, though he came scads of chads closer to occupying 1600 Pennsylvania Avenue than did the perennial Prohibition Party presidential candidate Earl Dodge, who once serenaded me with his party's theme song in a fourth-floor room of the Bucks County Sheraton in Langhorne, Pennsylvania:

> *I'd rather be right than president*
> *I want my conscience clear*
> *I'll firmly stand for truth and right*
> *I have a God to fear*
> *I'll work and vote the way I pray*
> *No matter what the scoffers say*
> *I'd rather be right than president*
> *I want my conscience clear*

Not to worry, Earl.

Pat Moynihan was sometimes right but never president, either. As for his conscience . . . ah, do I wonder.

Has there been an American politician as complex and contradictory as Senator Daniel Patrick Moynihan? He was an Irish Catholic yet a foppish Anglophile. He had the head of a reformist intellectual and the heart of a working-class regular. Certainly he was the only Harvard social scientist who could be greeted with backslapping beer-buying bonhomie in a Buffalo bar. The product of a broken home, Moynihan was courageous and far-sighted in analyzing the disastrous consequences of illegitimacy and the fracturing of the two-parent family.

A New Deal/Fair Deal Democrat who seldom voted against a government appropriation, Moynihan was a gimlet-eyed critic of the welfare state and, in his creative dotage, a practical decentralist of the kind no longer found in the Democracy. He believed in international law, magnificent public architecture, and labor unions. He delivered ramblingly learned extemporaneous speeches on recondite subjects while running shrewdly effective campaigns. He detested platitudes yet read the *New York Times*. He was a superb pork-barrel pol disguised as the absent-minded professor. He voted with the liberals but provided talking points to the conservatives. He trimmed, he temporized, he compromised, he was cowardly when the times (if never the *Times*) demanded valor. He left no legislative mark. He is irreplaceable.

Not only was Moynihan a deft dipper in the pork barrel, he was also among the savviest pols of his age. Consider 1982, the only year in which the Republicans did not write off the race against incumbent Moynihan as unwinnable before it even started.

By far the weakest candidate in the Republican field—Assemblywoman Florence Sullivan—was nominated over her wealthy opponents, Muriel Siebert and Whitney North Seymour. The primary results were a shocker. How did the pathetically underfunded Sullivan come up with the funds to pay for a last-minute mail blitz that was generally credited with putting her over the top against her deep-pocketed foes? One might almost suspect the invisible hand of Moynihan—but no, a Mugwump would never do such a thing.

Moynihan trounced Sullivan, winning two-thirds of the vote—despite being targeted by the New York branch of the Moral Majority, as the senator pointed out in a stupendously silly observation. He'd have whipped the early Republican front-runner by an even handier margin: Former Rep. Bruce Caputo, the presumptive GOP nominee, dropped out of the race after newspaper reports—fed by Moynihan-staff leaks—revealed that he had manufactured a military record for himself. Caputo was lucky: more, ah, personal revelations were forthcoming had he received the nomination.

The professor played hardball. Or at least he hired men who knew how to play.

So much nonsense has been written about Moynihan over the years. He was the absent-minded professor, lost in lofty cerebration, neglecting grubby politicking, blah blah. In fact, most of the books he published during his Senate years were ghostwritten by staffers. (Every biennium I enjoyed the line in Michael Barone's *Almanac of American Politics* in which Barone cluelessly confided, "He is one senator who reads widely and—his ornate style leaves no doubt—writes his own speeches and articles.") Moynihan's courage failed him at critical moments, not only in his refusal to stop the Senate candidacy of non–New Yorker Hillary Clinton but in his last-minute retreat from what would have been a headline-making— perhaps even career-breaking—act of conscience on the matter of abortion. From Pat Moynihan I learned, among other things, the soul-corroding effect of cowardice.

Daniel Patrick Moynihan, the most prominent politician-professor since Woodrow Wilson, was born not in a firetrap tenement to a shanty colleen but in Tulsa, Oklahoma, to a father who was a jaunty drunk and newspaper reporter (or do I repeat myself?) and a mother from one of the most prominent families in Jeffersonville, Indiana. Father John took a job as an advertising copywriter at RKO and moved the family to the Stygian nothingness of the New York suburbs. His drinking and whoring and erratic behavior spun out of control until finally he fled to San Jose (yes, he did know the way), leaving his emotionally unstable wife Margaret and the kids to a transient life in a series of coldwater flats in the upper 80s and lower 90s of Manhattan.

Choked in the interstices between the precarious middle class and the downwardly mobile working class, the Moynihans bounced from Queens to Manhattan to suburban New Jersey. The senator's myth-makers, himself included, liked to say that he came of age in Hell's Kitchen, though Ed Koch amended that to "Hell's Condominium."

In lurches and purposeful staggers, young Moynihan made his way, as well as his myth. Stevedore. City College scholar. Bohemian sailor who loved jazz and was nicknamed . . . Jellyroll? Two-fisted Tufts grad student. Chatty aide to Governor Averell Harriman. Convivial wit in a series of administrations, Democrat and Republican, until in 1976 he stabbed that main chance good and hard, winning a crowded U.S. Senate Democratic primary and then trouncing incumbent James Buckley.

Moynihan was a young man of the left, a reader of Erskine Caldwell, with a pugnacious populist streak. His prep school friends, he announced, needed "a good swift kick in their blue blood asses. They need to get hurt once in a while. They need to get some feeling in them."

He was a Tertium Quid in the New York politics of the 1950s and early '60s: his head agreed with the reformers, but his heart belonged to Tammany, to the ass-kicked and ass-kicking ethnic Catholics who had not gone to college, who had never read Sartre, and whom "the liberals, al-most exclusively a middle- and upper-class group," held in contempt.

Pat Moynihan had the rare talent to blend Mugwumpery, with its commitment to honest and open government and its perhaps naïve faith in meritocracy, to a distinctly anti-Mugwump disposition. He would write trenchant position papers for the blue bloods whose asses he had just kicked. Alas, rare is the flower that can reach its fullest efflorescence in the soot and stink of Gotham.

The great tragedy of Pat Moynihan's life was that his toper dad dragged the family out of Oklahoma. Had the Moynihans remained in Tulsa, young Pat could have matured in a healthy American environment, far from the Trotskyist miasma settled over the CUNY cafeteria. In retro-spect, there is a depressing inevitablity in his evolution toward standard-issue Cold War liberalism. He had a visceral hatred of parlor pinks, so he was a reflexive anticommunist, mistaking—as did some of the others with whom he briefly pitched the tent of neoconservatism—unconditional sup-port for the projection of U.S. military might for authentic patriotism. Domestically, he seems to have viewed the New Deal–Fair Deal regulatory state as the only feasible alternative to outright socialism—but then on the grimy streets and in the feculent air of his youthful haunts, those *were* the only choices presented to a boy not clad in silk stockings.

Had he been raised an Oklahoman, Pat Moynihan might have become a towering populist leader, a William Jennings Bryan of our very own. Imagine a Moynihan weaned on Alfalfa Bill Murray, far from the Harrimans and Kristols. A Moynihan whose temperament would have led him, naturally, to a Jeffersonian populism with deep roots in even the most desiccated tumbleweed acre. Yet a Moynihan sophisticated enough to avoid the snares that claim the cruder populists—a sinful racism, in particular.

Alack, we will have to be satisfied, or not, with the Moynihan we got. I have written elsewhere of his martinet qualities. He was a wretched boss, as I learned in my two-and-a-half-year stint (1981–83) as a research assistant and then legislative assistant to a man every bit as worthy as Webster had been of bearing the sobriquets "the Godlike Daniel" and "Black Dan." By the time my comet streaked across the Moyniverse, the Senate's only dairy farmer, as he absurdly called himself, was down to his last few drops of the milk of human kindness. He was the drunkenly petulant verification of Henry Adams's aphorism that "No man, however strong, can serve ten years as schoolmaster, priest, or Senator, and remain fit for anything else." And Henry should know.

One of the oldest practices in the political burlesque is exaggerating one's closeness to Powerful Men. The classic example is Sinclair Lewis's *The Man Who Knew Coolidge*, in which a blowhard on a train bores his seatmates with intimate tales about a president whom he bumped into on a college green decades ago. I am not quite so bumptious a fool—almost, but not quite.

I had not expected my own Moynihan Story to have a touching— well, at least *touched*—ending. But it did. For I saw him almost a score of years after I had shuffled out of the Russell Senate Office Building for the last time, the senator's eyes not beclouded by tears at a parting of which he was perhaps dimly aware. Our reunion was over a weirdly delightful and drunken three-hour lunch in Syracuse just months before the deathdew lay cold on his brow.

My friend Karl Zinsmeister and I had not seen the old browbeater in nineteen years. We expected him to mistake us for the bellboys, since one servant is pretty much the same as the next to a Senate lifer, but he was downright . . . dare I say avuncular?

"Lads, how a-bout a *drink*!?" he chirped as we shook hands in the lobby of the downtown Syracuse Sheraton. The bar was dark, as bars usually are at 10:45 a.m., but the tapster's meek protest of "we're not open till noon" was no match for Pat Moynihan in full thirst. The bar opened early.

Karl is a teetotaler, so I did my Irish-quadroon best to keep up with the senator, though I dropped out at four glasses of pinot grigio (his matutinal nectar). We spoke of many things that day, from the dream of an independent Brooklyn to the obduracy of New Yorkers who support a leviathan that means his state harm to his somewhat befuddled pride in the Moynihan alumni (Tim Russert and a cast of dozens) made good, or at least semi-famous. It's as if dear old Dad, after 20 years of bummin' and slummin' and an absence that made no hearts grow fonder, wakes to find his child delivering the high school valedictory address. How in hell did *that* happen?

As the glasses of wine emptied, the speech slurred, the eloquence dimmed. References to 9/11 became "7-11," as if bin Laden had declared jihad against Slurpees. And yet even in the wine-darkened noontide of a Syracuse hotel bar, the past was present. Our rambling chat was interrupted by a middle-aged black man who with a hybrid French-Irish accent represented himself as a former Black Panther. "Patrick Moynihan!" he boomed in a patois brogue, and after a hearty handshake and cordialities about the '60s, "when I was way over there, on the other side," he took his leave, with a theatrically whispered and mischievous farewell: "Benign Neglect, Patrick. Benign Neglect!"

Moynihan never could outrun that artless expression. It had been three decades since he had used the phrase in a confidential memo to President Nixon in which he proposed a moratorium on new racial initiatives; torn out of context, "benign neglect" was used to suggest that Moynihan was anti-black. The libel never died. In fact, it would cripple him in largely unseen ways. Moynihan had been so shaken by the reaction to the Nixon memo, and his earlier 1965 report to President Johnson on the instability of the black family, that he swore off race matters, spending his Senate career uttering the sort of numbing platitudes that, however unworthy of a serious man, do keep Democratic primary challengers at bay. Moynihan, unlike Eugene McCarthy, took to heart Gore Vidal's puckish maxim: "The price of freedom is eternal discretion."

And yet in the bibulous twilight of his career, his insights grew keen. He toyed with a radical decentralism, wondering aloud (though no one listened) whether or not most functions of the federal government ought to be turned back to the states and cities. He called for the abolition of the CIA, the return of American troops from Europe, and a foreign policy redolent of Oklahoma rather than Manhattan. (Moynihan would have been greatly amused a while back, when New York drivers received letters from the Department of Motor Vehicles advising us that our "Liberty plates" were to be replaced by "Empire plates." Symbolism weighs heavy, even from the bumper of an automobile.)

One of the strangest rituals in the U.S. Senate is the annual reading of Washington's Farewell Address. The chore of recitation usually falls to a freshman nonentity eager to curry favor by performing what is regarded as a drudge task. The chamber is empty, save for the sole classical relict: West Virginia Democrat Robert Byrd, the pomaded knight from the mountaineer state, who with his florid defenses of the U.S. Constitution against the PATRIOT Act, the Iraq War, the line-item veto, and the effluvium of Big Government Republicanism has earned himself a place in Valhalla.

Pat Moynihan used to be there, too, taking in the bizarre sight of some junior Honorable stumbling through Washington's injunctions against "overgrown military establishments" and "permanent alliances with any portion of the world" and "excessive partiality for one foreign nation," the last of which, Washington warned, leads to a black-is-white inversion wherein "real patriots who may resist the intrigues of the favorite are liable to become suspected and odious."

After this perfunctory nod, the Senate spends the next 364 days of the year repudiating the Father of Our Country. But it's the thought that counts, right?

In his dotage, Moynihan strayed from the pack and started flying with the Byrd—if not eight miles high, then at least far enough above the ground to see dimly the outlines of the wreckage of the Old Republic.

He began to use pejoratives like "national security state" and "military-industrial complex." True to Washington's dictum about avoiding permanent alliances, by 1993 he was calling for a complete withdrawal of U.S. troops from Europe. The Cold War, he insisted, was history. "It's over! It's over!" he thumped to *Newsweek*.

He and Pat Buchanan are the only two American politicos who seem to have rethought matters in the wake of the Soviet Union's dissolution. Both well-read Irish Catholics, distinctive literary stylists . . . well, the kinship only goes so far. But it's there. Like Buchanan, Moynihan took a deep breath and a long look and came up radical and reactionary. In 1991 he proposed to abolish the Central Intelligence Agency, which had been "repeatedly wrong about the major political and economic questions entrusted to its analysis." (He would transfer intelligence gathering to the Department of State.) His "End of the Cold War Act of 1991" sought to shine light on the intelligence budget and sharply curtail the ability of the executive to bar visitors on ideological grounds—proposals unthinkable a decade later, in the age of Homeland Security.

Like Buchanan, Moynihan eloquently opposed the First Gulf War, and in Gene McCarthyite language he mused, "I find it extraordinary . . . that the President should so personalize the encounter with this particular thug in Baghdad: the most recent thug in Baghdad, not the last by any means. There will be others." He warned of a "permanent crisis," of what the revisionist historian Harry Elmer Barnes and Gore Vidal have called "perpetual war for perpetual peace."

The enemy "used to be totalitarian, Leninist, communism. Without a moment's pause almost, we shifted the enemy to this person at the head of this insignificant, flawed country whose boundaries were drawn in 1925 in a tent by an English colonial official. . . ."

By his last decade, not only had he gone anti-imperialist, he had also lost his New Deal faith in centralization, consolidation, and bigness. Since 1977, his first year in the Senate, Moynihan had published a report on "New York State and the Federal Fisc," in which he documented New York's balance of payments with the federal government. The exercise had its pork-barrelish aspect—we used its annual finding that New York is shortchanged to argue for altered formulae, special grants, and other means of raining alms on the Empire State. But by 1991, in the fifteenth—or, rather, XVth—edition of the Fisc, Moynihan had recanted. Though since no one ever bothered to read the Fisc, least of all those journalists forever bemoaning the lack of substance in American politics, it went unnoticed.

The Senator asked if it might be

time we began to ask just how much a bargain Federal programs are for a state such as New York? I know. This is heresy. Since the time of Theodore Roosevelt, at very the least, New Yorkers have consistently supported an expansion of the programs of the Federal government. As, for example, the first Roosevelt's Bureau of Reclamation, which has brought such bounty to 17 Western states. Decade after decade, New Yorkers have been thinking up new Federal programs. The Interstate Highway System, for example, a concept of the second Roosevelt. In the beginning these were often inspired and hugely successful programs. Rarely, however, did we look to our particular interest. The Interstate system is the perfect example. New

York built its own principal segment of the system as a toll road; then paid gas taxes to build the same toll-free road all over the rest of the country. The years since have seen one such instance after another, even if there have been no New York Presidents. <u>New Yorkers can be counted on to support Federal programs that redistribute resources away from New York.</u> We manage to get back a share of Federal outlays proportionate to our population. But with a higher nominal income we continuously, systematically send resources elsewhere. Worse yet, what money does come back more and more comes back loaded with restrictions and strictures that New Yorkers would never adopt on their own. Call it the Jesse Helms effect, named for my good friend, the senior Senator from North Carolina.

Moynihan goes on to examine the case of education, federal aid to which has long been a cornerstone of New York's suffocating bipartisan consensus: "[A]fter a generation of Federal aid, and Federal preachment about education, New York hasn't got a lot to show. Is it wrong to ask whether we would have done better to have kept our money and energy at home?" To ask the question is to answer it. Pat Moynihan had placed himself, by 1992, far to the decentralist "right" of his party on domestic issues and just as far to its antiwar "left" on foreign policy. He was as far out of the party's mainstream, and as deeply set in his country's main grain, as Eugene McCarthy. Like McCarthy, he was an independent liberal.

But no one paid any mind. A year and a half later, Bill Clinton, a neoliberal Democrat whom Moynihan despised, was president. The senator, who by 1992 was calling himself a "Mugwump," would go into fitful opposition, especially to Clinton's Rube Goldberg health-care proposal. Like maverick California Democrat Jerry Brown, Moynihan floated a cut in the regressive Social Security payroll tax. But he prized too much the headpats and medals of the Establishment to follow Al Smith's path of Democratic dissent.

Al Smith had been the last puissant force for decentralism in the New York Democracy. Smith viewed himself as a defender of "the traditional role of the Democratic Party, which has been since the days of Jefferson the party opposed to highly centralized Federal control."

Like Moynihan, Smith had a genuine feeling for life, and tenderness, on the block. Yet the modern nepenthe has erased any national memory of this progressive Democrat who despised FDR as callow and shallow and spent his declining years as smiling front man for the pointless Empire State Building.

Smith's womb had been St. James parish and Manhattan's Fourth Ward, close-knit communities whence he derived a politics of subsidiarity. Like Moynihan, Smith's staff was Jewish-Catholic, an eclectic mix ranging from the Alabama-born Jewish states-rights liberal Joseph Proskauer to the pestiferous Robert Moses, who would later raze the neighborhoods Smith eulogized.

Moses ought never to be mentioned in polite company without a parenthetical fustigation. No man more perfectly embodied Imperial New York than Robert Moses, who from a series of official and quasi-official perches spent half a century paving, razing, and evicting with grim ruthlessness. Moses built the expressways that scarify the five boroughs and the bridges that connect them: in all, he was responsible for an incredible 627 miles of road in and around New York City. Like the suburban federal judge who destroys working-class neighborhoods with busing orders, Moses sat blissfully distant from the wrack and ruin of his acts. The bastard never even learned how to drive. Not that such ignorance has ever deterred New Yorkers from telling *others* how to drive. For years, the speed limit on upstate highways was set at a ridiculously low fifty-five miles per hour due to a bloc of Gotham legislators who didn't know a clutch from a kvetch.

In *The Power Broker* (1974), the utterly devastating biography of Moses which appeared shortly before its subject died—making it a heartwarming example of a bad guy getting his just desserts on *this* side of Hades—author Robert Caro figured that the number of people evicted by Moses's highways plus urban renewal and building projects was "close to half a million."

"He tore out the hearts of a score of neighborhoods, communities the size of small cities themselves, communities that had been lively, friendly places to live, the vital parts of the city that made New York a home to its people," wrote Caro. Remarkably, most of those people moved with no more resistance than a grumble: living in Imperial New York had made them pliant and spiritless.

That Al Smith was patron to young Moses is as inexplicable as Elton John belting out "Saturday Night's Alright for Fighting."

"I would sooner be a lamp-post on Park Row than the Governor of California," said Al Smith with hale parochialism. His latest biographer quails at this "horrible line," but it embodies much of what made Al Smith Al Smith and not, say, Mario Cuomo. It explains why Governor Smith, a first-class loather of communism, bravely vetoed noxious Red Scare measures calling for loyalty tests for teachers, the licensing of private schools, and the removal of radical parties from the ballot. A man who knows his neighbors does not see bogeys under every bed.

The parallels with Moynihan go a respectable ways. Smith was wet in theory (he signed the repeal of the mechanism by which New York enforced prohibition), Moynihan was wet in, ah, practice. Despite their liberalism, neither was ever trusted by feminists, Smith for especially good reason: he, like many Catholics, was lukewarm at best toward woman suffrage. He belittled the Equal Rights Amendment, remarking, "I believe in equality, but I cannot nurse a baby." To the extent such a thing can be measured by terrene observers, Smith was the more devout Catholic, and his papistry was a factor—but just a factor, for 64 of his 87 electoral votes came from the allegedly anti-Roman South—in his landslide loss to Herbert Hoover in 1928. (As the gag went, the night of the election the pope received a one-word telegram: "Unpack.")

No one ever accused Pat Moynihan of taking orders from the Vatican. He broke with the church when it was politically expedient for him to do so, and he never found the moxie to reverse course. In the late 1980s, Moynihan prepared a declaration of what would have been a stunning volte-face on the most undiscussable of subjects: abortion, or as the corporate media have redubbed it, "choice." It was in the form of a letter to the cardinal apologizing for his pusillanimity, his previous inability to break ranks with Democratic pro-choice orthodoxy and cast the pro-life votes impelled by his church and his own belief. The letter was never sent; he was talked out of it by an adjutant for the obvious political reasons.

I did not see the letter. Of course it makes no appearance in Godfrey Hodgson's donnishly hagiographic *The Gentleman from New York* (2000). Nor will it likely complicate the narrative of any future Moyni-bio. I believe only two or three persons ever saw what would have been among the most reviled or admired epistles in recent political history. The man who told me this story contemporaneously—an absolutely impeccable source— remains active in liberal Democratic politics. He would deny it if you asked him about it. But it happened.

The closest Moynihan ever got to repudiating the NARAL line was when he described partial-birth abortion as "infanticide." The choicers looked at him askance, but only for the nonce, for the debate was one of those sound-and-fury distractions over largely factitious "issues" that have not a blessed thing to do with how we live now. Breaking ranks over a (gruesome) sideshow: this is what passes for iconoclasm in a conformist age.

In our chat shortly before his death, I asked the senator if there was "a place today for pro-life Irish Catholics in the Democratic Party." He was pretty well plastered by this time, but through the wine-dark haze he murmured, "I have not gotten over the denial of Governor [Robert] Casey (D-PA) [to speak before the Democratic Convention] in 1992. I thought that was shameless. It almost made me start voting differently."

Almost. And Scott Norwood's right leg *almost* won the Super Bowl for Buffalo. When Pat Moynihan might have changed the terms of debate, he was silent.

(Lest I be accused of that inconsistency which is the hobgoblin of small minds, I should mention that I oppose any and all abortion legislation, pro or con, at the national level, and would see its legality determined at the most local level possible.)

The habit of caution so necessary to a sustained political career breeds, ineluctably, gutlessness, even among those who cultivate a reputation for straight shooting.

I once interviewed Lyn Nofziger, one of those true-believing Reaganauts who followed their Ron from Sacramento eastward. After I turned the tape recorder off, he told me that while he was publicly supporting publishing heir Steve Forbes for president, privately he was pulling for Pat Buchanan. I felt such an immense surge of pity mixed with contempt that I wanted to vomit over his suburban Virginia cowboy boots. The habit of circumspection, of cowardice masquerading as caution, of dissimulation, had become so much a part of Nofziger—the alleged wild man of the Reagan administration, the straight shooter, the no-bullshit bulwark of candor—that even in his pasturage, far removed from the corridors of power, in a station in which absolutely no one gave a damn what he thought, he was incapable of supporting an old friend if that friend had crossed the GOP authorities.

Nofziger had written a series of pleasant page-turning Westerns in the Louis L' Amour mode. No doubt he imagined himself Gary Cooper, but I left that D.C. high-rise thinking him a lot closer to Bob Hope in *Paleface*.

Lyn the Niddering, meet Pat the Caitiff. Like most Democrats who had come of age with postwar internationalism, Moynihan was a convinced free trader. Yet he voted protectionist. He once told me, "This must never become law"—fine, but he was speaking of a domestic-content bill that he had *cosponsored*. In the early 1980s, he voted a straight ADA liberal line, a record that can be explained, in part, by Moynihan's nettling fear that he was going to wake up in 1944 and have to contend with a spirited challenge from Vito Marcantonio and the American Labor Party.

Similarly, Pat Moynihan detested the Clintons, but once Hillary declared her candidacy for his seat never was heard a discouraging word about that paragon of placelessness. He kept quiet, and the press kept gushing.

And what does a lifetime of sedulously kissing up to Sulzbergers get you? Two days before Hillary Clinton was elected U.S. senator from New York despite never having resided in the Empire State, the *New York Times Magazine*, which Gore Vidal once called "that graveyard of prose," but which had been theretofore a reliable producer of Moynihan-the-lovable-drunk-professor boilerplate profiles, published "For the Sake of Argument," in which Jacob Weisberg tore into the superannuated DPM as a "magnificent failure," a maundering blowhard lost in "irrelevance and self-regard" who "lacked the largeness of spirit necessary to transcend his animosities." His once charmingly idiosyncratic prose style had degenerated into "self-absorbed baroque." (Or could it simply be that Moynihan wrote better Moynihanese than did his staff ghosts?)

Moynihan was out of power, out of luck, even out of favor. Still, he parried all of our questions about Hillary, the faithful party man till the end. He was willing to pop off on matters far removed from party lines, however, and in fact from out of left field came the single headline resulting from our talk.

I asked Moynihan, "Would Brooklyn have been better off remaining an independent city?" and he blurted, "Yes. Like Minneapolis-St. Paul."

Brooklyn, the erstwhile "city of homes and churches," fourth-largest city in the union, dissolved itself into the Blob via the pivotal 1894 referendum, its citizens voting to join the City of New York by a vote of 64,744 to 64,467. But testing Daniel Webster's dictum that "[b]ecause a thing has been wrongly done, it does not follow that it can be undone," dreamy secessionist sons of Brooklyn from Pete Hamill to Norman Mailer have sought to divorce their beloved mother from that foul old lech across the river. Moynihan, it seems, had joined them.

Upon its publication in the *American Enterprise*, his answer stirred a brief controversy: East Harlem City Councilman Charles Barron raged to the *New York Sun*, "I just hope the author of 'benign neglect' is not once again coming up with some plan based on the changing demographics" of largely non-white Brooklyn. His colleague Simcha Felder said that it didn't matter if an independent Brooklyn was poorer on its own: "Brooklyn would have to live with the fact that it was just richer in people and culture." Now that's a patriot.

Felder is echoed by Jane Jacobs, the vastly influential urban writer: "Brooklyn and the other boroughs would all be better off on their own. . . . Big bureaucracies can't allow for the diversity and the experimentation that are essential to cities." Who but the most obdurate imperialist can possibly take exception to that?

And who but the most humorless ideologue could be unmoved by Pat Moynihan, if only for the magnificence of his failure? I am—no, a piece of me is—one of those ethnic Catholic Democrats whose tribune Moynihan sometimes wished to be but was not. But I laugh still at the thought of the roistering drunken Irishman who secretly wishes to take tea with the Queen. Yeah, sure, he mythicized his labor as a stevedore on the waterfront, but I composted my own toil as a factory janitor cleaning the most fetid men's rooms imaginable. His staff was overwhelmingly Ivy League yet he declared that "a party of the working class cannot be dominated by former editors of the *Harvard Crimson*." And hell, he hired me. As a Western New York localist, I admire him as the only statewide politician within my lifetime to have a sympathetic understanding of Upstate New York. Moynihan could descant, off the cuff and on the bottle, on the history of the Erie Canal or the significance of Seneca Falls. And he could be bluntly funny. In a 1961 essay in *Commentary*, he called Buffalo a "big, ugly, turbulent city." I asked him if that un-Chamber of Commerce-ish description ever caused him problems in his campaigns. He looked at me incredulously, then asked, "How many people in Buffalo do you think read *Commentary*?"

One would be too many, senator. One would be too many.

My two-and-a-half years in the employ of Senator Moynihan were an anarchist-making experience. I came to Washington a memorizer of senatorial facts, a skeptically cheerful liberal, a first-time voter in the year past for Ted Kennedy and John Anderson for president, an awestruck walker through august halls of state; I left quoting the mid-century anarchist Frank Chodorov: "A government building you regard as a charnel house, which in fact it is; you enter it always under duress, and you never demean yourself by curtsying to its living or dead statuary. The stars on the general's shoulders merely signify that the man might have been a useful member of society; you pity the boy whose military garb identifies his servility. The dais on which the judge sits elevates the body but lowers the man, and the jury box is a place where three-dollar-a-day slaves enforce the law of slavery. You honor the tax dodger. You do not vote because you put too high a value on your vote."

Mind you, my profuse and sentimental localism keeps me from being half as radical as Chodorov. I have friends who are judges, legislators, even soldiers. I vote often, if futilely. I pay town, village, and county taxes without grumbling. (I've a mild objection to state taxes, and I loathe, execrate, and abominate—but pay—federal taxes, which are put to purposes nefarious and even homicidally sinister.)

Pat Moynihan's name is emblazoned across a Manhattan train station and an Institute of Global Affairs at Syracuse University. Eugene McCarthy was an eponym manqué. Dorothy Day, the Catholic subject of the next chapter, had politics closer to those of the Jewish agnostic Frank Chodorov than to Pat Moynihan. Unlike Moynihan, she hadn't any wish to "rise above" her circumstances, her neighborhood, her place. But then she was a saint, while Pat Moynihan, even if occasionally on the side of the saints, was loyal, finally, to another party altogether.

CHAPTER TWO

The Way of Love

The American Distributism of Dorothy Day

"The Virgin and St. Thomas are my vehicles of anarchism. Nobody knows enough to see what they mean, so the Judges will probably not be able to burn me."

—HENRY ADAMS

I write next of a Catholic far more reactionary—and radical—than either McCarthy or Moynihan: Dorothy Day, a woman "haunted by God" who lived the gospel through the hospitality houses in which she and her Catholic Workers fed, clothed, and befriended the poor. The anarchist Day practiced her Christianity so consistently that she smilingly explained to impatient socialists that she was "a pacifist even in the class war."

On the centenary of Dorothy Day's birth, I gave a talk at Marquette University on the subject of "Dorothy Day and the American Right." Given that Day is a heroine of what the feverish minds on the anticommunist right used to call "the far left," this promised to be a mercifully brief exposition, along the lines of "Commandments We Have Kept" by the Kennedy brothers. After all, the founder of the Catholic Worker movement and editor of its newspaper lived among the poor, refused to participate in air-raid drills, and preferred Cesar Chavez to Bebe Rebozo. A pacifist, her idea of military reform was military abolition. What could she possibly have in common with the American Right?

Nothing, if the Right in question is the barbed-wiretapped world of the Department of Homeland Security. But just as there is more to the

"Left" than the bureau-building and bomb-dropping of Roosevelts and Kennedys, so is the Right rather more complex than a mere dollar bill stretching from Reagan to the Bushes. Dorothy Day, finally, belonged to neither left nor right, but in her life and her good works, which in due time will bring formal recognition of the sainthood evident in her daily acts, Day was the compleat anarchist: the perfect harmonizing of the best features of "left" and "right."

The Catholic reactionary and historian John Lukacs, after attending the lavish twenty-fifth anniversary bash for *National Review* in December 1980, held in the Plaza Hotel, hellward of the Catholic Worker house on Mott Street, wrote:

> During the introduction of the celebrities a shower of applause greeted Henry Kissinger. I was sufficiently irritated to ejaculate a fairly loud Boo! . . . A day or so before that evening Dorothy Day had died. She was the founder and saintly heroine of the Catholic Worker movement. During that glamorous evening I thought: who was a truer conservative, Dorothy Day or Henry Kissinger? Surely it was Dorothy Day, whose respect for what was old and valid, whose dedication to the plain decencies and duties of human life rested on the traditions of two millennia of Christianity, and who was a radical only in the truthful sense of attempting to get to the roots of the human predicament. Despite its pro-Catholic tendency, and despite its commendable custom of commemorating the passing of worthy people even when some of these did not belong to the conservatives, *National Review* paid neither respect nor attention to the passing of Dorothy Day, while around the same time it published a respectful R.I.P. column in honor of Oswald Mosley, the onetime leader of the British Fascist Party.

National Review, dreadnought of postwar American conservatism, occasionally aimed its scattershot at Day. Founder William F. Buckley Jr. referred casually to "the grotesqueries that go into making up the Catholic Worker movement"; of Miss Day, he chided "the slovenly, reckless, intellectually chaotic, anti-Catholic doctrines of this good-hearted woman—who, did she have her way in shaping national policy, would test the promise of Christ Himself, that the gates of Hell shall not prevail against us."

The grotesqueries he did not bother to itemize; nor did Buckley—whose magazine's most memorable witticism was *Mater, Sí, Magistra, No!*—explain just what was "anti-Catholic" about a woman who told a friend, "The hierarchy permits a priest to say Mass in our chapel. They have given us the most precious thing of all—the Blessed Sacrament. If the Chancery ordered me to stop publishing *The Catholic Worker* tomorrow, I would."

If this is anti-Catholicism, then Buckley's limousine has a NASCAR sticker on its bumper. Dorothy Day, and humane anarchists in general, befuddle ideologues. She may have been a puzzlement to Buckley and Kissinger, but there is another right—or is it a left, for praise be the ambidextrous—in which Miss Day fits quite nicely. Indeed, she is more at home with these people than she ever was with Manhattan socialists. They are the Agrarians, the Distributists, the heirs to the Jeffersonian tradition. The keener of them—particularly the Catholics—understood their kinship with Day. Allen Tate, the Southern man of letters and contributor to the 1930 Southern Agrarian manifesto *I'll Take My Stand*, perhaps the central influence on a later generation of traditionalist conservatives, wrote his fellow Dixie poet Donald Davidson in 1936:

> I also enclose a copy of a remarkable monthly paper, *The Catholic Worker*. The editor, Dorothy Day, has been here, and is greatly excited by our whole program. Just three months ago she discovered *I'll Take My Stand*, and has been commenting on it editorially. She is ready to hammer away in behalf of the new book. Listen to this: *The Catholic*

Worker now has a paid circulation of 100,000! [Tate neglects to say that the price is a penny a copy.] ... She offers her entire mailing list to Houghton-Mifflin; I've just written to Linscott about it. Miss Day may come to Nashville with us if the conference falls next weekend. She has been speaking all over the country in Catholic schools and colleges. A very remarkable woman. Terrific energy, much practical sense, and a fanatical devotion to the cause of the land!

The program that so excited Miss Day was summarized in the statement of principles drawn up at the Nashville meeting of Southern Agrarians and Distributists. Mocked as reactionary for their unwillingness to accept bigness as an inevitable condition, the conferees declared (*inter alia*):

— The condition of individual freedom and security is the wide distribution of active ownership of land and productive property.
— Population should be decentralized as well as ownership.
— Agriculture should be given its rightful recognition as the prime factor in a secure culture.

Though Day was absent from Nashville, she was to speak the language of the Southern Agrarians, without the drawl, many times over the years. "To Christ—To the Land!" Day exclaimed in the January 1936 issue. "*The Catholic Worker* is opposed to the wage system but not for the same reason that the Communist is. We are opposed to it, because the more wage earners there are the less owners there are. ... [H]ow will they become owners if they do not get back to the land[?]"

Widespread ownership was the basic tenet of the Agrarians' Catholic cousins, the Distributists. The *Catholic Worker* published all the major

Distributists of the age, among them Chesterton and Belloc, Fathers Vincent McNabb and Luigi Ligutti, and the Jesuit John C. Rawe (a Nebraska-based "Catholic version of William Jennings Bryan"). On numberless occasions Dorothy Day called herself a Distributist. Thus her gripe with the New Deal: "*Security* for the worker, not ownership," was its false promise. She despaired in 1945 that "Catholics throughout the country are again accepting 'the lesser of two evils' . . . They fail to see the body of Catholic social teaching of such men as Fr. Vincent McNabb, G. K. Chesterton, Belloc, Eric Gill and other distributists . . . and lose all sight of *The Little Way*."

The Little Way. That is what we seek. That—contrary to the ethic of personal parking spaces, of the dollar-sign god—is the American way. Dorothy Day kept to that little way, and that is why we honor her. She understood that if small is not always beautiful, at least it is always human.

———————

The Catholic Worker position on economics was visionary, idealistic, and utterly untainted by Marxism or capitalism:

> [W]e favor the establishment of a Distributist economy wherein those who have a vocation to the land will work on the farms surrounding the village and those who have other vocations will work in the village itself. In this way we will have a decentralized economy which will dispense with the State as we know it today and will be federationist in character . . . We believe in worker ownership of the means of production and distribution as distinguished from nationalization. This is to be accomplished by decentralized cooperatives and the elimination of a distinct employer class.

The American name for this is Jeffersonianism, and the failure of Distributism to attract much of a stateside following outside of those H. L. Mencken derided as "typewriter agrarians" owes in part to its Chesterbellocian tincture. "Gothic Catholicism" never could play in Peoria.

Nor could it stand upon the Republican platform. Garry Wills recalls this exchange during his first visit with Buckley: "'Are you a conservative, then?' [Buckley asked.] I answered that I did not know. Are Distributists conservative? 'Philip Burnham tells me that they are not.' It was an exchange with the seeds of much later misunderstanding."

Were the Distributists conservative? Was Day conservative? Depends. Herbert Agar, the Kentucky agrarian and movement theorist, wrote in the *American Review* (April 1934), "For seventy years, a 'conservative' has meant a supporter of Big Business, of the politics of plutocracy," yet "[t]he root of a real conservative policy for the United States must be redistribution of property." Ownership—whether of land, a crossroads store, a machine shop—must be made "the normal thing."

"Property is proper to man," insisted Dorothy Day, though she and the Distributists—and much of the Old American Right—meant by property something rather more substantial than paper shares in a Rockefellerian octopus. "Ownership *and* control are property," declared Allen Tate, making a distinction between a family farm—or family firm—and a joint-stock corporation, the artificial spawn of the state.

Like Tate and the Southern Agrarians, Day was no collectivist, eager to herd the fellaheen onto manury unromantic Blithedales. "The Communists," she said, sought to build "a sense of the sacredness and holiness and the dignity of the machine and of work, in order to content the proletariat with their propertyless state." So why, she asked, "do we talk of fighting communism, which we are supposed to oppose because it does away with private property[?] We have done that very well ourselves in this country." The solution: "We must emphasize the holiness of *work*, and we must emphasize the sacramental quality of *property* too." ("An anti-religious agrarian is a contradiction in terms," according to Donald Davidson.)

Day described the Catholic Worker program as being "for owner-ship by the workers of the means of production, the abolition of the assembly line, decentralized factories, the restoration of crafts and the ownership of property," and these were to be achieved by libertarian means, through the repeal of state-granted privileges and a flowering of old-fashioned American voluntarism.

During the heyday of modern American liberalism, the 1930s, when Big Brother supposedly wore his friendliest phiz, Dorothy Day and the Catholic Workers said No. They bore a certain resemblance to those old Progressives (retroprogressives, really)—Senators Burton K. Wheeler (D-MT), Gerald Nye (R-ND), and Hiram Johnson (R-CA)—who turned against FDR for what they saw as the bureaucratic, militaristic, centralizing thrust of his New Deal. Bishop Muench of Fargo, North Dakota, who was sympathetic to the agrarian left, expressed these concerns when he warned Catholics in October 1941 that "governmental control and regimentation are winding their octupus [sic] tentacles tighter and tighter around every phase of our national life. American democracy is developing into totalitarian democracy."

The antithetical tendencies of the *Catholic Worker* and the '30s American Left were juxtaposed in the November 1936 issue of the CW. Under the heading "Catholic Worker opposition to Projected Farm-Labor Party," the box read:

Farm-Labor Party stands for:	*Catholic Worker stands for:*
Progress	*Tradition*
Industrialism	*Ruralism*
Machine	*Handicrafts*
Caesarism (bureaucracy)	*Personalism*
Socialism	*Communitarianism*
Organizations	*Organisms*

And never the twain shall meet.

In the flush and heady first year of Mr. Roosevelt's Caesarism, Day's comrade, the clochard Peter Maurin, reasoned:

> 1. People go to Washington, asking the Federal Government to solve their economic problems, while the Federal Government was never intended to solve men's economic problems.
> 2. Thomas Jefferson says: "The less government there is the better it is."
> 3. If the less government there is, the better it is then the best kind of government is no government.

An anarchistic distrust of the state, even in its putatively benevolent role as giver of alms, pervaded the Catholic Workers. But then as Karl Hess, onetime Barry Goldwater speechwriter turned Wobbly homesteader, wrote, the American Right had been "individualistic, isolationist, decentralist—even anarchistic," until the Cold War reconciled conservatives to the leviathan state.

The 1930s dissenters—the old-fashioned liberals now maligned as conservatives; the unreconstructed libertarians; the cornbelt radicals—proposed cooperatives and revitalized village economies as the alternative to government welfare. The Catholic Workers agreed. Peter Maurin asserted that "he who is a pensioner of the state is a slave of the state." Day, in her memoir *The Long Loneliness*, complained: "The state had entered to solve [unemployment] by dole and work relief, by setting up so many bureaus that we were swamped with initials . . . . Labor was siding in the creation of the Welfare State, the Servile State, instead of aiming for the ownership of the means of production and acceptance of the responsibility that it entailed."

"Bigness itself in organization precludes real liberty," wrote Henry Clay Evans Jr. in the *American Review*, a Distributist journal. The home—the family—was the right size for most undertakings. And so the home must be made productive once more. In the April 1945 *Catholic Worker*, Janet Kalven of the Granville Agricultural School for Women in the exquisitely named Loveland, Ohio, called for "an education that will give young women a vision of the family as the vital cell of the social organism, and that will inspire them with the great ambitions of being queens in the home." By which she did not mean a sequacious helpmeet to the Man of the House, picking up his dirty underwear and serving him Budweisers during commercials, but rather a partner in the management of a "small, diversified family farm," who is skilled in everything "from bread-making to bee-keeping." For "the homestead is on a human scale"—the only scale that can really measure a person's weight.

The agrarians and Distributists dreamed of achieving a (voluntary, of course) dispersion of the population, and Day, despite her residence in what most decentralists regarded then and now as the locus of evil, agreed: "If the city is the occasion of sin, as Fr. Vincent McNabb points out, should not families, men and women, begin to aim at an exodus, a new migration, a going out from Egypt with its flesh pots?" asked Day in September 1946. This revulsion against urbanism seems odd in a woman whose base was Manhattan, symbol of congestion, of concentration, of cosmopolitanism rampant. Yet she wrote of the fumes from cars stinging her eyes as she walked to Mass, of the "prison-gray walls" and parking lots of broken glass. "We only know that it is not human to live in a city of ten million. It is not only not human, it is not possible."

The Southern agrarians would not demur.

Yet if to the outsider, New York City is vast, monstrous, inhuman, Dorothy Day discovered in her little piece of it what Chesterton called "that splendid smallness which is the soul of local patriotism."

In March 2002, Geoffrey Gneuhs, who eulogized Day at her 1980 funeral and did double duty as CW chaplain and as an editor of the *Catholic Worker* newspaper, kindly walked me around the Worker world. Geoffrey is an accomplished painter whose subjects include Day, CW regulars, and the shops and scenes of his neighborhood in the East Village. He is deepset in the Catholic Worker tradition; he is also active in the Sons of the American Revolution and has affinities for the political right, or that part of the right that believes in decentralizing political power. Like Mailer, he is something of a "left conservative." (Stormin' Norman named a daughter after Dorothy Day.)

The Worker clientele is changing. The face of Christ, which looked like toothless Irish winos and grizzled layabouts in Dorothy's day, has become younger, darker, and more likely to belong to a junkie than a drunk.

At one of the Worker houses, I read a wall-tacked memorial for "Sister" Jeanette Chin, a "holy fool" in the unambiguously favorable meaning of the phrase. Sister Jeanette, who had died the previous year at the age of 70, was a touched (by God?) old streetlady with a somewhat irregular habit of wearing a nun's garb—despite the technicality that she never did take the vows.

The Workers are fond of epigrams. To Sister Jeanette's picture is appended her favorite saying, and a fine one it is: "I vote for Jesus because Jesus votes for everybody." RIP, Sister—even though Jesus would get creamed in a citywide election. A pro-life extremist can't win in New York, you know.

Neither can a working Catholic—or a Catholic Worker. Even Dorothy Day was ripped off by Robert Moses. The city condemned one of the Worker homes as a sacrifice to the god of efficient transportation. Yet in keeping with the old Catholic teaching about the immorality of usury, the Workers returned the interest that had accumulated on the city's eminent domain payment. In accepting only the principal, they retained their principles.

World War II destroyed agrarianism as an active force in American intellectual life just as it fortified the urban citadels of power and money. Foes of U.S. involvement in the war, heirs to the noninterventionist legacy of

George Washington, were slandered, most notably Charles Lindbergh, whom the *Catholic Worker* defended against the smears of the White House.

Despite Day's disavowal of the "isolationist" label, the *Catholic Worker* of 1939–41 spoke the diction of the American antiwar movement, which, because it was anti-FDR, was deemed "right wing." Sentences like "We should like to know in just what measure the British Foreign Office is dictating the foreign policy of the United States!" could have come straight from the pages of Colonel McCormick's *Chicago Tribune*. So could the paper's objection to the "*English and Communist propaganda*" of the New York papers, and its advocacy of the traditional "neutrality of the United States," which meant keeping "our country aloof from the European war."

"The *Catholic Worker* does not adhere to an isolationist policy," editorialized the paper in February 1939, though in fact its stance, and often its phraseology, bore the American isolationist signet. The editorial sought to distinguish the paper from the bogeymen "isolationists" by urging "that the doors of the United States be thrown open to all political and religious refugees"—a position also taken by many isolationists, for instance H. L. Mencken, who wanted our country to be a haven for the persecuted Jews of Europe.

Day and the Workers dug in for a tooth-and-nail fight against conscription—"the most important issue of these times," as they saw it. Day replied to those who noted that Joseph and Mary went to Bethlehem to register with the census that "it was not so that St. Joseph could be drafted into the Roman Army, and so that the Blessed Mother could put the Holy Child into a day nursery and go to work in an ammunition plant."

Or as Peter Maurin put it:

> The child does not belong to the state; it belongs to the parents.
> The child was given by God to the parents; he was not given by God to the state.

This was by now a quaintly reactionary notion. What were children if not apprentice soldiers? Like their isolationist allies, the Catholic Workers suffered years of "decline, suspicion, and hatred" during the Good War. Circulation of the *Catholic Worker* plummeted from 190,000 in May 1938 to 50,500 in November 1944. By 1944, only nine of thirty-two Houses of Hospitality were operating.

The Cold War transmogrified the American Right. Anticommunism became its warping doctrine, yet a remnant of cantankerous, libertarian, largely Midwestern isolationists held on, although the invigorating air of the 1930s, when left and right might talk, ally, even merge, was long gone. The fault lies on both sides.

The unwillingness of the *Catholic Worker's* editors to explore avenues of cooperation with the Old Right led them, at times, to misrepresent the sole popular anti-militarist force of the late 1940s. In denouncing the North Atlantic Treaty which created NATO, the *Catholic Worker* claimed that "the only serious opposition in the Senate is from a group of the old isolationist school, and their argument is that it costs too much." This is flatly untrue—the isolationist case was far more sophisticated and powerful, and it rested on the same hatred of war and aggression that inspirited the Catholic Workers—but to have been honest and fair would have placed the CW on Elm Street and Oak Street, whose denizens might have taught the boys in the Bowery a thing or two.

Listen to Nebraska Republican Congressman Howard Buffett, stalwart of the "far right" in the House of Representatives (and father of the investment guru Warren Buffett), excoriate the Truman Doctrine: "Our Christian ideals cannot be exported to other lands by dollars and guns. Persuasion and example are the methods taught by the Carpenter of Nazareth. . . . We cannot practice might and force abroad and retain freedom at home. We cannot talk world cooperation and practice power politics." Then hear Dorothy Day ask, "[W]hat are all these Americans, so-called Christians, doing all over the world so far from our own shores?" Which is the Catholic Worker and which is the isolationist?

To call the retroprogressive journalist John T. Flynn an exponent of "semi-fascism," as Michael Harrington did in the *Catholic Worker* (November 1951), is both odious and ignorant, and it suggests that the blindness, the refusal to see beyond the prison cells labeled "left" and "right," afflicted Catholic Worker eyes as well. (Flynn, parenthetically, was among the tangiest critics of the maldistribution of wealth in our country; in 1956, he was expelled by Mr. Buckley from *National Review* for submitting an essay lacerating the "racket" of militarism.)

Postwar Catholic isolationists were condescended to as parochial morons by the Cold War–liberal likes of James O'Gara, managing editor of *Commonweal*. O'Gara snickered at these mossbacks who refused to recognize that "American power is a fact" and that "[m]odern science has devoured distance and made neighbors of us all." What good is personalism in a world of atomic bombs? What mattered the small? Father John C. Rawe's experimental school of rural knowledge, Omar Farm, near Omaha, was shattered when all but two of its students were drafted to fight World War II. Liberal Catholics continued to support the conscription against which pacifists and isolationists railed, although, as Patricia McNeal has written of the League of Nations debate, "the majority of American Catholics supported the popular movement towards isolationism and rejected any idea of collective security." But the League aside, we all know which side won. The state side. The liberals who do not know us but, as they so unctuously assure us, have our best interests at heart.

"The greatest enemy of the church today is the state," Dorothy Day told a Catholic audience in 1975, sounding much like the libertarian right that was her natural, if too seldom visited, kin.

The powerful libertarian strain in the *Catholic Worker* was simply not present in other postwar magazines of the "left," excepting *politics*, edited by Day admirer Dwight Macdonald. American liberals had made peace with—had made sacrifices to—Moloch on the Potomac. As *Catholic Worker* editor Robert Ludlow argued in 1951:

> [W]e are headed in this country towards a totalitarianism
> every bit as dangerous towards freedom as the other more
> forthright forms. We have our secret police, our thought
> control agencies, our over-powering bureaucracy. . . . The
> American State, like every other State, is governed by those
> who have a compulsion to power, to centralization, to the
> preservation of their gains. And it is the liberals—the *New
> Leader, New Republic, Commonweal* variety—who have
> delivered the opiate necessary for the acceptance of this
> tyranny among "progressive" people. It is the fallacy of
> attempting social reform through the State, which builds
> up the power of the State to where it controls all avenues
> of life.

To which the *New Republic*–style liberals replied: Welcome to the real world.

The inevitable Arthur Schlesinger Jr., in *The Vital Center* (1949), his manifesto of Cold War liberalism, wrote, "One can dally with the distributist dream of decentralization," but "you cannot flee from science and technology into a quietist dreamworld. The state and the factory are inexorable: bad men will run them if good abdicate the job."

Alas, most on the "right" crawled into the devitalizing center. A dispersion of property, a restoration of ownership, the reclaiming of the land, a foreign policy of peace and noninterference: these were the dreams of losers, of fleers from reality, of shirkers of responsibility. Of—most damningly—*amateurs*. Non-experts. In 1966, in the just-as-inevitable *National Review*, Anthony T. Bouscaren mocked Day and other "Catholic Peaceniks" because, "sinfully, [t]heir analysis of the situation [in Vietnam] goes directly counter to that of the distinguished list of academicians . . . who support U.S. defense of South Vietnam." Grounds for excommunication, surely.

In all this worry about the other side of the world, few partisans bothered to notice the dirt under their feet. Distributism was dead. Or was it? For in 1956, long after the agrarian dream had been purged from the American Right, supplanted by the Cold War nightmare, Dorothy Day insisted that "distributism is not dead." It cannot "be buried, because distributism is a system conformable to the needs of man and his nature."

Consistent with their decentralist principles—and presaging a later strategy of "right-wing" tax resisters—the Workers refused payment of federal taxes, although as Day wrote, we "file with our state capital, pay a small fee, and give an account of monies received and how they were spent. We always comply with this state regulation because it is local—regional" and "because we are decentralists (in addition to being pacifists)." These actions, she explained, were "in line with common sense and with the original American ideal, that governments should never do what small bodies can accomplish: unions, credit unions, cooperatives, St. Vincent de Paul Societies. Peter Maurin's anarchism was on one level based on this principle of subsidiarity, and on a higher level on that scene at the Last Supper where Christ washed the feet of His Apostles. He came to serve, to show the new Way, the way of the powerless. In the face of Empire, the Way of Love."

What a beautiful resolve. In the face of Empire, the Way of Love.

It is only in the local, the personal, that one can see Christ. A mob, no matter how praiseworthy its cause, is still a mob, said Day, paraphrasing Eugene V. Debs, and she explained, in Thoreauvian language, her dedication to the little way:

> Why localism? . . . [F]or some of us anything else is
> extravagant; it's unreal; it's not a life we want to live. There
> are plenty of others who want that life, living in corridors
> of power, influence, money, making big decisions that affect
> big numbers of people. We don't have to follow those
> people, though; they have more would-be servants—slaves,
> I sometimes think—than they know what to do with.

We don't happen to believe that Washington, D.C., is the moral capital of America. . . . If you want to know the kind of politics we seek, you can go to your history books and read about the early years of this country. We would like to see more small communities organizing themselves, people talking with people, people *caring* for people. . . . We believe we are doing what our Founding Fathers came here to do, to worship God in the communities they settled. They were farmers. They were craftspeople. They took care of each other. They prayed to God, and they thanked Him for showing them the way—to America! A lot of people ask me about the influence on our [Catholic] Worker movement, and they are right to mention the French and the Russian and English writers, the philosophers and novelists. But some of us are just plain Americans whose ancestors were working people and who belonged to small-town or rural communities or neighborhoods in cities. We saw more and more of that community spirit disappear, and we mourned its passing, and here we are, trying to find it again.

Dorothy Day found it. Not on the left, and not on the right, but in that place where Love resides. In the face of Empire, the Way of Love.

CHAPTER THREE

Return from Bohemia

Grant Wood and the Promise of American Regionalism

"America, turn in and find yourself."

—PAUL ENGLE

So there we were, my wife, Lucine, our then-nine-year-old daughter, Gretel, and I, driving the gravel roads outside Clear Lake, Iowa, following directions like "first fencerow past the big grain bin," till we ditched the rental car and walked the narrow half-mile path between corn and soybean fields to the spot where on February 3, 1959, the plane carrying Buddy Holly, Ritchie Valens, and the Big Bopper crashed, a tragedy later mythicized by Don McLean in "American Pie" as "the day the music died." We found the cross and makeshift memorial to the three paleo rock-and-rollers. Lucine detests the har-har leering of the Big Bopper— "Hell-ooooooo Ba-Beeeee!"—but Gretel and I persuaded her to join us in a spirited chorus of "Chantilly Lace," capped by a hearty "Oh baby that's what I like!" I imagined the Bopper, a bespangled specter, giving us a lewd wink.

If an Iowa farm is the place where the music died, Iowa writ large is also where the music—American music—was born, and where, in chapbooks of poetry and gleaming brass bands and well-tended graveyards (for everything that dies someday comes back, as a New Jersey regionalist once sang), we find the seeds and pith and guts of a real American culture, as opposed to the unreal America of the TV screen, the ABC-Fox-HBO axis of vile.

In the summer of 2003 we took a cultural tour of the Upper Midwest. Three slaphappy ghouls in a rent-a-car, watching independent baseball in North Dakota and grave-hopping from Sauk Centre, Minnesota (Sinclair Lewis), to Anamosa (Grant Wood), Mason City (Meredith Willson), and West Branch, Iowa (Herbert Hoover).

Our pilgrimage coincided with the annual "Sinclair Lewis Days," run by Lewis's bête noire, the Chamber of Commerce, and featuring a Miss Sauk Centre beauty pageant and a pool tournament. Lewis would have loved it. His headstone in the family plot in Greenwood Cemetery looks out on the new Morningview Drive development, where we may be sure George W. Babbitt IV is chuckling at Jay Leno, boasting of the high school's new array of computers, and wishing that Sauk Centre would attract a Home Depot.

If our cemetery-tripping seems morbid, North Dakota's Timothy Murphy asks:

> Why are we born with tongues
> if not to praise the dead?

The dead, we may be sure, are under no obligation to praise us. Indeed, I rather expect the shade of Buddy Holly was cursing the cacophony as we shouted our eulogy in that Clear Lake cornfield.

Clear Lake, coincidentally, was the site of Grant Wood's last studio. The painter's spectacles were every bit as unhip as Buddy Holly's; Miss Prescott, the Cedar Rapids principal who against all logic gave the absent-minded Wood a teaching job at a critical point, said he "looked dumb." Slow, halting of speech, geekish in his Devo glasses and goofy gadgets (when making a left turn with his car he stuck out a carved hand with a pointing index finger), Wood, by standing on what he stood for, stood foreground when last American artists might treat American themes with Jeffersonian eye.

Grant Wood was of Quaker stock on his father's side and Upstate New York matrilineage—a happy combination conducive to a cautious radicalism. He displayed an almost evangelical zeal in promoting the culture of the Midwest, and specifically Iowa, not as cloying encomiast but as a lovingly gimlet-eyed native son. His Iowa regionalism, at once populist and conservatively agrarian, imbued such iconic paintings as *American Gothic* as well as his long-forgotten but sophisticated and practicable plan for a "revolt against the domination exercised over arts and letters and over much of our thinking and living by Eastern capitals of finance and politics." Wood, Thomas Hart Benton, and John Steuart Curry, the Midwestern triumvirate of that golden movement and moment known as "Regionalism," were being echoed by many writers, among them the dozen Southern agrarian authors of *I'll Take My Stand* and the unreconstructed Tennessee poet and charter Southern agrarian Donald Davidson in his gallant *Attack on Leviathan* (1938).

Henry Wadsworth Longfellow, in his charming novel *Kavanagh* (1849), told of a writer manque in a small New England village whose tales of the exotic and foreign never quite made the transmutative transit from imagination to pen:

> What Mr. Churchill most desired was before him. The Romance he was longing to find and record had really occurred in his neighborhood, among his own friends. It had been set like a picture into the frame-work of his life, enclosed within his own experience. But he could not see it as an object apart from himself; and as he was gazing at what was remote and strange and indistinct, the nearer incidents of aspiration, love, and death, escaped him. They were too near to be clothed by the imagination with the golden vapors of romance; for the familiar seems trivial, and only the distant and unknown completely fill and satisfy the mind.

Grant Wood escaped Mr. Churchill's myopia. Or should we say he was saved from it by an epiphany. Upon returning from one of several trips to Europe, Wood saw "*like a revelation*, my neighbors in Cedar Rapids, their clothes, their homes, the pattern of their tablecloths, the tools they used. . . . I suddenly saw all this commonplace stuff as art, wonderful material."

Like American regionalists from Sarah Orne Jewett to the Beach Boys, Wood made myth of the sand 'neath his feet.

Countee Cullen might "marvel at this curious thing/ To make a poet black, and bid him sing!" but even more marvelously curious is the artist who lives among, even sells to, his neighbors, his subjects. Wood's lifelong friend Marvin Cone, also an Iowa artist of distinction, noted, "The best testimony as to how his home folks liked him is the widespread ownership of his work in this community, not only in homes, but in offices and in industry."

Wood decorated Turner Mortuary; made a series of paintings of workers at Cherry-Burrell, a manufactory of dairy equipment; and drew Cedar Rapids historicana—its first trading post, a wood-burning fire engine. He painted murals for hotels in Sioux City, Waterloo, Cedar Rapids, and Council Bluffs. He was that rare artist who was fully a citizen of his place.

Behold Grant Wood chatting up the delegates at an Iowa convention of the National Selected Morticians Association (with an early Maecenas, funeral director Dave Turner); building sets for Cedar Rapids community theater and taking supernumerary parts; and trying to create an artists' colony first in Cedar Rapids, then Stone City (where he met John Steuart Curry), which lasted two glorious years (1932–33).

Elementally, one might say, Wood founded Stone—Stone City, that is, on ten acres among limestone quarries whose veins would be bled for art, not profit. In a brochure advertising Stone City, Wood called upon "all midwestern painters" to strive "toward the development of an indigenous expression."

He wished to see Iowa ablaze with local color. Dr. Elizabeth Halsey of the University of Iowa recalled, "When Grant established a Saturday afternoon critique of amateur paintings, he held it in one of the medical amphitheaters. Anyone—town or country, student or housewife—who wanted his work reviewed was welcome to bring it. And anyone who wanted *to listen*, could come."

"I am a loyal Iowan and love my state," he explained. To modern ears, Wood may sound cornpone. I hear him as wholesomely seditious. For he believed in a truth that has become, in an age of American Empire and global culture, a heresy: Iowa matters.

Regionalism, it must be emphasized, was not jingoism, or flag-waving, or the painterly equivalent of the microwave-tortilla eater's "USA! USA!" chant croaked out during televised time-delayed Viagra-sponsored Olympic matches. Wood, in 1937, called regionalism "a revolt against cultural nationalism—that is, the tendency of artists to ignore or deny the fact that there are important differences, psychologically and otherwise, between the various regions of America." (Confounding posterity, the loquacious Benton, something of a cultural nationalist himself, tended to "explain" regionalism without the regions: "Together, we stood for an art whose forms and meanings would have direct and easily comprehended relevance to the American culture of which we were by blood and daily life a part . . .")

Wood's extraordinary manifesto "Revolt Against the City" (1935) was his clearest statement of regionalist principles. The pamphlet was published in Iowa City by Frank Luther Mott, who served as the model for Wood's illustration of "The Booster" in the Limited Editions Club edition of Lewis's *Main Street*. This disgracefully neglected essay is among the most literate pieces ever to appear under the byline of an American artist. (Mott may have "edited" it, and I mean to invest those quotation marks with pregnancy.)

"America has turned introspective," Wood announces in "Revolt Against the City." The Great Depression has been salutary in reteaching

Americans "self-reliance," with its Emersonian echo. Deprived of national (which is to say New York–based) and international markets, American artists have fallen back upon themselves and the places that gave them nurture. Community theaters (in which Wood had been active) and regional playwrights were putting heretofore invisible American lives on stage; perhaps Vachel Lindsay's old dream of a decentralized American cinema was also aborning.

While his confreres Benton and Curry were careful to include urban America in the regionalist mix, Wood is skeptical. He draws the lesson that "cities were far less typically American than the frontier areas whose power they usurped"; riddled with European epigoni, "they were inimical to whatever was new, original and alive in the truly American spirit."

It is time, reckons Wood, to retire the fatigued cliché of the artsy young boy shaking the field dust from his boots and hightailing it to the cosmopolitan East Coast. "[T]hose of us who have never deserted our own regions for long find them not so much havens of refuge, as continuing friendly, homely environments." Iowa, for instance, is "not a drab country inhabited by peasants, but a various, rich land abounding in painting material."

Enter regionalism, whose "basic idea" is this: "Each section has a personality of its own, in physiography, industry, psychology. Thinking painters and writers who have passed their formative years in these regions, will, by care-taking analysis, work out and interpret in their productions these varying personalities. When the different regions develop characteristics of their own, they will come into competition with each other; and out of this competition a rich American culture will grow."

America, Wood understood, was the sum of its regions. Homogenization, globalization, the concentration of power: these are the enemies of American art. What happens if Boise and Chapel Hill shop, watch, and listen in the same way? Can any art beyond a pallid universalism emerge from the transient suburbanite whose experiences are bounded by Target, Taco Bell, and the films of Mike Nichols?

Wood thought not.

So far, so good. But at this point Wood puts away his brush and picks up his metaphorical GS card. Complications ensue. You see, Grant Wood was "a New Dealer before there was a New Deal," according to Hazel E. Brown, a classmate of Wood and Marvin Cone at Washington High School in Cedar Rapids and author of a brief but illuminating remembrance of her coevals titled *Grant Wood and Marvin Cone: Artists of an Era*. Wood was an Iowa Democrat of progressive leanings and an admirer of Henry Wallace, whom he depicted for a *Time* cover, though in practice his Rooseveltism left something to be desired. For like Edmund Wilson, Wood simply forgot to pay income taxes over a stretch of years. Magazine writers find this a hoot, but paying tribute to the central state is the kind of thing that seldom occurs to a freeborn American of the Wood-Wilson grain, no matter how such men vote. Perhaps the limits of the New Deal revealed themselves to Wood when the Internal Revenue men showed up at his house asking where his 1935, '36, and '37 reports might be.

Wood was, in fact, a New Deal employee, albeit in attenuated form. As director of the Public Works Art Project in Iowa, he oversaw the painting of federally subsidized murals in the Hawkeye State. His experience led him to propose, in "Revolt Against the City," federal sponsorship of regional arts centers.

> The germ of such a system for the United States is to be found in the art work recently conducted under the PWA. The Federal Government should establish regional schools for art instruction to specially gifted students in connection with universities or other centers of culture in various sections. . . . The annual exhibits of the work of schools of this character would arouse general interest and greatly enlarge our American art public. A local pride would be excited that might rival that which even hard-headed business men feel for home football teams. . . .

We'll forgive Grant his superabundant optimism.

The forty-year experience of the National Endowment for the Arts does not inspire confidence in Wood's vision of a state-tended blooming of thousands of distinct and local flowers. In his classic study *The Democratic Muse* (1984), Edward Banfield pointed to the "problems of political geography" manifest when small-city museums use federal eleemosynary to purchase works "mostly from New York City artists." Banfield concluded, "The real reason for the passage of the act [creating the NEA] and for the making of appropriations year after year was, and is, to benefit special interests, especially the culture industry of New York City."

I once had great fun drawing up various bills of indictment against the NEA, cutting the gyves off my Gothamophobia and populism and letting them run free. Anecdotes of NEA grantee superciliousness are as numerous as grains of sand in the seashore. For our purposes, one will suffice: when George Plimpton paid Aram Saroyan $1,500 for a poem consisting of the single misspelled word "lighght," an Iowa congressional aide dared ask the dilettantish Plimpton what the poem meant.

"You are from the Midwest. You are culturally deprived, so you would not understand it anyway," replied the New Yorker Plimpton, whose enduring contribution to American letters is a football book (*Paper Lion*) not half as good as the contemporaneous edited diaries of a Green Bay Packer lineman (Jerry Kramer's *Instant Replay*.)

But I fight no more under an anti-NEA flag. When Dana Gioia, the superb Northern California poet who in a bureaucratic fluke was nominated by George W. Bush to head the arts agency, asked me to serve on the National Endowment for the Arts "FY 2005 Local Arts Agencies: Access to Artistic Excellence" panel, I flipped my inner ideologue the finger and said okay. (To assuage my conscience, I donated the small stipend to local civic groups.) And though I voted against the final package on the grounds that eight of the fifteen agencies that made the cut were from New York or California, I was much impressed by the caliber of the relatively skeletal endowment staff. Not for the first time was I flummoxed by the collision between ideology and people as they really are. Though I am no more philo-sophically attuned to the National Endowment for the Arts than I ever was, I no longer care to lend hand or epithet to the anti-NEA side. Of all the criminal or unconstitutional acts of the U.S. government in the age of Empire, sending paltry thousands of dollars to favored museums, sympho-nies, small presses, and even tediously transgressive trust-fund artists is a sin so venial as to vanish into our thinning air.

Yet I still think Wood was mistaken to propose federal subsidy of regional arts centers. For how can state-supervised cultural cells tend to-ward anything other than tyranny or (more likely in the U.S.) a crushing mediocrity? The painter John Sloan, when asked in 1944 what he thought about a Federal Bureau of the Arts (to complement Mr. Hoover's Federal Bureau of Investigation?), replied, "Sure, it would be fine to have a Minis-try of the Fine Arts in this country. Then we'd know where the enemy is."

Besides, the two great efflorescences of American letters—in the 1850s and 1920s—occurred during decades of peace, governmental in-activity, and reviled "weak" or "below average" presidents such as Fillmore, Pierce, Harding, and Coolidge. Might culture profit from an enfeebled state? Might artists need not subvention, or direction from above, or gov-ernment checks in the mail, but simply to be left alone? Henry Thoreau would say so. His doggerel could have been penciled in response to the NEA's Guidelines for Grantees:

> *Any fool can make a rule*
> *And every fool will mind it.*

The regionalist dream has lasted a very long time—some of us have yet to wake from it. It predates world wars, even the Civil War. It has raged perfervidly in North and South, on the sidewalks of Brooklyn as well as in Sweet Home Alabama. Sang one antebellum New Yorker:

> Ere long, thine every stream shall find a tongue
> Land of the many waters!

The poetical prophet was Charles Fenno Hoffman, author of the best poem ever written upon a dead dog. You think I jest? On matters canine, never. Judge for yourself:

Epitaph Upon a Dog

> An ear that caught my slightest tone,
> In kindness or in anger spoken;
> An eye that ever watch'd my own,
> In vigils death alone has broken;
> Its changeless, ceaseless, and unbought
> Affection to the last revealing;
> Beaming almost with human thought,
> And more—far more than human feeling!
>
> Can such in endless sleep be chill'd,
> And mortal pride disdain to sorrow,
> Because the pulse that here was still'd
> May wake to no immortal morrow?
> Can faith, devotedness, and love,
> That seem to humble creatures given
> To tell us what we owe above,—
> The types of what is due to Heaven,—
>
> Can these be with the things that were,
> Things cherish'd—but no more returning,

And leave behind no trace of care,
 No shade that speaks a moment's mourning?
Alas! my friend, of all of worth
That years have stolen or years yet leave me,
I've never known so much on earth,
 But that the loss of thine must grieve me

I don't know about you, but I'm still bawling. And as long as we're on the subject of Hoffman, let us digress for just a moment . . .

Charles Fenno Hoffman, eulogist of dead dogs, was a one-legged Hudson Valley lawyer who had earned his gimp when, in a fit of boyish daredeviltry, he tried to leap from a pier onto a steamer. He came up about half a leg short. As he later came up short in his most ambitious project: a campaign to give our country a new name. If poets ran this land, Hoffman would be revered today as the father of our beloved Allegania.

Antebellum American poets felt keenly the infelicity of "United States." What could we call ourselves? "United Stateser" is hopelessly clumsy, and rhymes only with "late, sir" and "fate, sir." Besides, there were five other United Stateses in the hemisphere. "American," which—not to spoil the ending of this tale—won out, was imprecise, encompassing two continents and many countries.

Washington Irving had worried this bone for years. "We want a national name," wrote the keeper of Sunnyside. "We want it poetically, and we want it politically. . . . I leave it to our poets to tell how they manage to steer that collocation of words, 'The United States of America,' down the swelling tide of song, and to float the whole raft out upon the sea of heroic poesy." A stirring name "would bind every part of the confederacy together," predicted Irving.

So in March 1845, the New York Historical Society appointed Charles Fenno Hoffman, Indian expert Henry R. Schoolcraft, and attorney David Dudley Field to come up with a better name for their country. By month's end, their report was in. (Commissions worked faster in those days.) It urged replacing the "irrelevant appellation at present used for this country" with one "more likely to promote national associations, and prove efficient in History, Poetry, and Art."

The trio looked for a name in "our mountains, or our lakes, or our rivers." The Rockies they judged too distant; the northern lakes peripheral; the great Mississippi River and its tributaries had already given names to six states.

Taking a cue from Washington Irving, they settled upon "Allegania," to be pronounced "Algania" for poetical reasons. (Though suitable rhymes do not quite cascade: Mania? Mauritania? That's vain o' ya?)

The Alleghany Mountains were "the grandest natural feature of the country," declared Hoffman and company; "one that is common to the north and south; . . . the back-bone of the original thirteen states: and the dividing ridge between the Atlantic rivers and the great central valley of the continent." Moreover, the national monogram—USA—would be unchanged in a United States of Allegania.

The name speaks of "colonial adventure, and revolutionary heroism"; its Indian derivation gives it a native quality that a corruption of Italian explorer Vespucci's forename just doesn't have.

The Society asked other state historical societies and "eminent citizens" to jump aboard the Allegania bandwagon; mapmakers and textbook writers were requested to designate our land as the "Republic of Allegania."

It would have been easier to move the mountains themselves than to move men on the subject of the national name. Washington Irving, of course, was for Allegania, but his fellow Hudson Valley eminence Martin Van Buren was against. Another ex-president, John Quincy Adams, was appointed chairman of a Massachusetts Historical Society committee to consider Allegania; uncharacteristically, the Bay State stayed out of the fray.

Newspapers were found on both sides of the issue, but then this was an age when poets—Allegania's chief constituency—published in the daily press, where they actually had readers. The *Boston Journal* was all for a new national name, but it preferred the infra dig "Yankee Doodle." The *Evening Gazette* of New York pointed out that westward expansion would render the Alleghany Mountains eccentric. The *New York Evening Post* published "Alleghania" by Henry B. Tuckerman, who (in addition to introducing a new spelling for the name) did his cause no favors with this example of the poetaster's art:

> *And Alps and Appenines resign their fame,*
> *When thrills the world's deep heart with Alleghania's name!*

In May 1845, Hoffman was shouted down at a raucous meeting of the New York Historical Society, at which his committee "hardly escape[d] without impeachment from these indignant United Statesers."

But that was to be the least of poor Hoffman's troubles. In 1848, a chambermaid accidentally used for kindling the manuscript of the nearly finished novel that he regarded as his masterpiece. Within a year, Hoffman suffered a nervous breakdown. He would spend the remaining thirty-five years of his life in and out of insane asylums, writing no poetry, the first forgotten mad poet in the Republic of Allegania.

What-ifs might litter our dreams, but then they also light the way back home. We could do worse than to heed our poets.

The Republic of Iowa has its own forgotten poets, mad or not. Quite sane was Jay G. Sigmund, a farmboy from Waubeek and vice president of Cedar Rapids Life Insurance Co. Like Grant Wood a native born to the banks of the Wapsipinicon River, Sigmund is often credited as the most clamant of those voices urging Wood to "paint America."

In best Wallace Stevens fashion, Sigmund combined his insurance career with poetry. He also wrote badly undervalued short stories that, while clearly animated by his enormous affection for the people of his home region, possessed little of quaintness and belonged instead to the Midwestern realist school of Edgar W. Howe, Sherwood Anderson, and Edward Eggleston.

Sigmund never traveled abroad and "seldom traveled beyond east-central Iowa." As poet Paul Engle eulogized him, "He wanted not an ivory tower but simply the water tower of his own village." A poet of corn, of herons, of Ridge Road women and huskers with bleeding hands, he extracted the holy and transcendent from the everyday. Wood read him, and he kenned Wood.

In 1937, Sigmund, an outdoorsman, died, Elmer Fuddishly, hunting wabbits. He had narrowly escaped death some years earlier in a more thematically apt accident. En route to the Stone City colony, where he was to serve as master of ceremonies for a Sunday variety show (no, neither the Beatles nor Topo Gigio were on the bill), the infrequent driver Sigmund rolled his car in a serious automobile accident later depicted by Wood in *Death on the Ridge Road*. (Cole Porter—Cole Porter?!; was any lad from Peru, Indiana, less likely to become a colporteur?—bought the painting.)

Grant Wood, like Jay Sigmund, never much liked automobiles, the primary instrument of dislocation. He disliked driving, and in *Death on the Ridge Road* he depicted them as deathtraps. Of persons, yes, but they would also consume a culture.

The automobile, and especially that grand Republican experiment in state socialism known as the National System of Interstate and Defense Highways, did so much to deface and distort the American mien. Sigmund, who after all made his comfortable living as an insurance man, was never auto-besotted:

> *Death used to ride a white-maned horse*
> *Before these gray roads lined the sod*
> *But now he travels on his course*
> *Astride a sleek thing, rubber-shod.*

The rubber-shod have brought only more shoddiness in the decades since. Tim Fay, publisher of the handsome and literate regional journal the *Wapsipinicon Almanac*, sees his redoubt of Anamosa—Grant Wood's hometown—under assault from the highwaymen. Fay recently told Iowa City's *Icon*: "People think [the new four-lane highway] is so great because it will bring all these people from Cedar Rapids who want to get their kids away from drugs and everything. But all it will mean is people coming to Anamosa to build these sprawl homes and make developers and real-estate people some money. They'll live here but go back to Cedar Rapids for their entertainment. They'll shop at Menard's, Wal-Mart and Hy-Vee. . . . And they're going to drive, keep driving and driving and driving and use more gas. But that's just what people want. They think that's the natural order of things. Nobody questions that."

The Iowa novelist Ruth Suckow, who wrote with artistry and understanding of her farm neighbors in the 1920s, called the Midwest "the seat of American complacency and the seat of American rebellion." For our beloved country's sake, let it now be the latter. May the unnaturalness of the "natural order" be revealed unto them.

The revelations might come from painters, from poets, though seldom, contra Vachel Lindsay, from politicians.

Lindsay, in imagining Abraham Lincoln taking on New York City, counseled:

> *Sing a Kansas love-song, modest, clean and true.*
> *Sing a Kansas love-song, modest, clean and true.*
> *Then lift your psalm of the Manna of our God!*
> *It is the only way to go into Babylon,*
> *Call down fire from Heaven, and the world renew.*

The Kansas love-song might be sung more convincingly by Grant Wood's partner in Regionalism, John Steuart Curry, who was likelier to call upon tornadoes than fire, and in any case when Curry found himself at the eye of the storm it was in Topeka, not Gotham.

John Steuart Curry, plowboy, was born outside Dunavant, Kansas, in 1897, when the Jayhawk state still raged with the prairie fires of agrarian revolt. A fine halfback on his high school football team, Curry was also one of the few noted American artists to treat football as a serious subject. (University of Wisconsin Coach Harry Stuhldreher, upon seeing Curry's 1938 oil sketch *End Run*, asked the artist, "When in the world did you ever see us run off a play where we managed to get that much interference in front of the runner?")

Curry met Wood at Stone City. Hazel Brooks recalled "John, who looked so much like Grant in height, width, shape of head and face, and rolypolyness." Call the diversity police!

Curry explained Regionalism, or "American Scene" painting, this way: "We are glorifying landscapes, elevated stations, subways, butcher shops, 14th Street, Mid-Western farmers, and we are one and all painting out of the fullness of our life and experiences." The artist admitted the urban potential in Regionalism, although his subjects were almost invariably rural: a country baptism, a roadmenders camp, a stockman, and always The Storm, whether in funnel clouds or lightning, chasing Kansans into cellars and riving oak trees. Thomas Hart Benton was less conciliatory—"The great cities are dead. They offer nothing but coffins for living and thinking"—but then he liked nothing better than sending into a tizzy the neurotic and neurasthenic Manhattanites who, then and now, set themselves up as the hall monitors of the art world.

An exile from the Plains, Curry lived for the better part of his adulthood in New York City, until in 1936 he took the novel position of Artist in Residence at the Agricultural College of the University of Wisconsin. The painter was "bald, jolly, pipe smoking, and liked to wear overalls," recalled his Wisconsin colleague Robert Gard, but Curry's affability was sorely tried when he learned that fundamental Scriptural truth: a prophet is ever without honor in his hometown. Or in this case, his home state.

For in 1937, one of those clusters of Leading Citizens Who Get Things Done raised the money to commission from Curry three murals for the state capitol in Topeka. "I want to paint the things I feel as a native of Kansas," said Curry, and those things ranged from covered wagons to John

Brown to sunflowers to the menacing tornadoes that seem always to spiral in Curry's skies.

The artist's early sketches for the project attracted statewide publicity and invited the sort of nitpicking that vexed Curry, whom his friend Benton described as "oversensitive to criticism." According to art historian Laurence E. Schmeckebier, Curry's Kansas "critics contended that pigs' tails do not curl when they eat; skunks' tails curl up over their backs when they walk and are not straight as he had painted them; or the red color of Curry's Hereford bull was too red and not 'natural-like.'" The conscientious Curry betook himself to a nearby hog farm, where he found that some pigs' tails do indeed curl when they eat. But he uncurled them anyway.

Yet artistic license was granted sparingly in 1930s Kansas: the porcine assault continued. One politically influential farmer complained that "them pigs look like they're on stilts; maybe they just waded out of the 1903 flood." The legs of Curry's cows were said to be too long. The skirts on his pioneer women were too short. Etcetera.

Despite the cavils—which might be seen as healthy civic involvement in public art—Curry completed two magnificent murals. The third, however, was never executed, for the Kansas legislature refused to remove panels of expensive Italian marble (ten bucks a square foot!) to make way for Curry's scenes of homesteading life.

Curry's carpers found the Italian marble a convenient rock with which to stone the artist. The Kansas Council of Women, announcing itself in favor of saving the marble, declared, "The murals do not portray the true Kansas. Rather than revealing a law-abiding, progressive state, the artist has emphasized the freaks in its history—the tornadoes, and John Brown, who did not follow legal procedure."

John Brown did not "follow legal procedure": ah, that Kansas gift of understatement!

So the last of Curry's three Kansas murals went undone. And the artist refused to sign those he had finished. Although Curry regarded the finished murals as "the greatest painting I have yet done," nevertheless the project was "uncompleted and does not represent my true idea."

If Curry did not exactly take Kansas by storm, it was not because he found such an ambition ignoble. He had written in *Art Digest* of his Iowa friend: "Grant Wood is producing an art that is real, indigenous to the life of his people. He has brought the town of Cedar Rapids and the state of Iowa renown and is, in my mind, the perfect example of . . . 'the artist as a part of his civilization.' Not only have the people of Cedar Rapids bought 400 of his pictures, but his advice is asked on the architecture and design of public buildings; the leading hotel is decorated by his hand."

Like Wood, Curry dipped his brush in the New Deal palette. He painted Federal Art Project murals in the Westport and Norwalk, Connecticut, high schools, as well as within the Departments of Justice and Interior in Washington. But he was not a bought man.

Curry's stepdaughter, wife of my late friend Dr. Dan Schuster of the University of Rochester, recalled in a 1969 interview of her mostly apolitical father: "Once he got angry at Franklin Roosevelt, and went tearing across the room and tripped on something and knocked the radio on the floor, so we were without communications for a while."

But in a roundabout way Roosevelt got the last word. For as Benton pronounced the eulogy upon Regionalism: "As soon as the Second World War began substituting in the public mind a world concern for the specifically American concerns which had prevailed during our rise, Wood, Curry, and I found the bottom kicked out from under us."

The Regionalist moment passed. Kansas, Iowa, and Missouri receded to the far fringe of the American artistic world. As if it were one of Curry's Kansas landscapes, the sky darkened, the clouds loured, the all-consuming vortex drew near. A pox was marked on all that was healthy in American life. Thomas Hart Benton knew their time was up: "The Museum of Modern Art, the Rockefeller-supported institution in New York, and other similarly culturally rootless artistic centers, run often by the most neurotic of people, came rapidly, as we moved through the war years, to positions of predominant influence over the artistic life of our country."

In E. Bradford Burns's marvelous *Kinship with the Land: Regionalist Thought in Iowa, 1894–1942* (1996), the concluding date is no arbitrary terminus: "In the years after 1942, internationalism, standards and life-styles prescribed elsewhere, and goals set by outsiders increasingly tri-umphed within Iowa. Like most regions of the United States, indeed of the world, Iowa was swept into a cultural homogeneity that on most levels denied the individuality of its own past and ignored those lively, percep-tive local voices that once called for introspection and valorization of the local."

The U.S. won the world war but lost Iowa.

Writes Burns: "After December 1941, one national goal exacted the full energy and attention of everyone: to defeat the Axis powers in Europe and Asia. The distant conflicts raised the eyes of all Iowans to new geo-graphical horizons. The war scattered the sons and daughters of Iowa to faraway places, requiring those who remained home to consult gazeteers in efforts to locate their whereabouts."

The die was cast. For the next six decades (and God knows how many more to come), Iowans looked away from Sioux City and learned to pronounce, if not understand, Seoul, Vladivostock, Phnom Penh, Fallujah. Burns concludes: "A significant victim of the world war was regionalism. The war eclipsed it."

After the deaths of Wood and Curry, Benton wrote, "The critics . . . just called us fascists, chauvinists, isolationists, and at the least, just igno-rant provincials." That a "regionalist fascist" is a contradictory impossibil-ity on the order of a "Christian atheist" did not faze the calumniators. For "isolationist" and "provincial" are the stigmata of Middle American cul-ture: they are deployed against any seditious local patriot who suggests that towns, neighborhoods, or provinces might generate their own cul-tures without the guidance of the placeless commissars of Manhattan, Washington, and Los Angeles. Because, you see, localism implies isolationism, which means peace, and that is the one thing we are never again to be allowed in the United States of Armaments. That and the conviction that, as art historian Joseph S. Czestochowski sums up the Regionalist ethos, "there was a permanence to be found in the values of rural America."

The Empire cannot abide the permanent things. Transience and rootlessness are its sacraments.

Regionalism extended into arts beyond painting. Curry's Badger colleague Robert Gard, yet another Kansas farmboy who found LaFollette's soil fecund, directed the Wisconsin Idea Theater and promoted the indigenous stage with such true-believing fervency that he was dubbed "the Johnny Appleseed of American grassroots theater" by August Derleth. (Derleth, in turn, had been hailed as a rising star of Upper Midwest letters by none other than Sinclair Lewis before turning his attention to occult fiction.)

Of course community theater is alive and well in the great American provinces today, with no little boost from my wife and daughter, but Gard's vision extended far beyond the Kenosha Players' production of "Hello, Dolly."

Gard the evangelist knew that "knowledge and love of place is a large part of the joy in people's lives. There must be plays that grow from all the countrysides of America, fabricated by the people themselves, born of their happiness and sorrow, born of toiling hands and free minds, born of music and love and reason. There must be many great voices singing out the lore and legend of America from a thousand hilltops. . . ." You may dismiss this as sentimental claptrap, windy populist hokum. I don't.

Neither did such Gardian angels as Alfred Arvold, founder of North Dakota's Little Country Theater, who in noblest North Dakota populist tradition rejected a proferred grant from the Rockefeller Foundation. (He who takes the king's shilling becomes the king's man.) Arvold was also the Imperial Potentate of the Nobles of the Mystic Shrine and thus one of the last—the only?—Shriners to play a prominent role in American theater.

The leading light of regional dramaturgy was an Upstate New Yorker, Alexander Drummond, born in William Seward's little city of Auburn and later director of the Cornell University Theater.

"He loved central New York above anything on earth," wrote Gard of Drummond, who also, he added, "holds his entire body more erect than any man I have ever seen."

Drummond dreamed of farmwife playwrights, of country-lawyer leading men, of hired hands washing off the shit and soil and sitting in converted barns watching autochthonous theater. He began staging rural productions at the 1919 New York State Fair, using Zona Gale's *The Neighbors*. Wisconsinite Gale offered usage of her play "without royalty in country theaters" as long as the cast agreed to plant a shade, fruit, or Christmas tree for every performance. Yes, these things really did happen once.

Drummond advertised in the *American Agriculturalist* to find rural Yorkers who wished to write plays about their hamlets, their farms, their histories, their feuds, their loves, their places. Taking a page from Zona Gale, he distributed these plays without demanding royalties. The Cornell University Theater performed more than forty of the works, and those he judged best were later published in *The Lake Guns of Seneca and Cayuga and Eight Other Plays of Upstate New York* (1942), a volume that suffers from rather too many plays by academics about rural life and too few by rural people about same. (Five of the nine were written or cowritten by Drummond or Gard.) But it was a start.

You can guess what killed Drummond's theater project. The same charnelhouse that killed off so many wholesome American projects, not to mention boys. The Good War. As Robert Gard wrote, "I might have lived and dreamed forever in the Finger Lakes country if it had not been for the war. But suddenly one day, there it was, and the course of our creative project in New York State was instantly altered. There was writing, yes, but it was frenzied writing on war-time themes, and when we looked about the land, there were no longer home-grown plays on country stages."

War. What is it good for?

"Luckily, eccentrics are tolerated, even encouraged, in small Iowa towns."

—W. P. KINSELLA, *THE IOWA BASEBALL CONFEDERACY*

Just fifteen miles southeast of the soybean field in which the music died marches Mason City, Iowa, the River City of *The Music Man*, the great American musical.

Music Man creator Meredith Willson checked into Mason City at fourteen pounds, six ounces, making him the biggest baby born in Iowa as of 1902. Perhaps that superfluous second "L" in his surname accounted for the avoirdupois.

Meredith—who hated his name as sissyish—was born to a Congregationalist Sunday School teaching mother and a real-estate lawyer father who had played baseball at Notre Dame and learned to throw a curveball from the inventor of that pitch, Candy Cummings. The family was not without those peculiarities—mom was churchy and opinionated, dad a hard-to-please sourpuss—often productive of an artistic temperament, and yet the activities of Meredith's boyhood were classically Middle American: playing cowboys and Indians, raising white mice, operating a lemonade stand.

The lad was mad for music. Other boys might wish to be Christy Mathewson or, in cases of extreme derangement, Woodrow Wilson, but Meredith adulated John Philip Sousa. A Sousa talent scout discovered Willson in Mason City, and the boy would tour with the King of Martial Marches for three years before joining Toscanini and the New York Philharmonic.

Shrewdly, Willson bet on a new medium, becoming West Coast musical director of NBC Radio. He composed, he conducted, he engaged in dopey prattle with the stars, including George Burns and Gracie Allen. He also referred "to Mason City, Iowa, at every possible opportunity," as a New York critic complained. The *Mason City Globe-Gazette* took to listing "Good News," one of his radio shows, as "The Meredith Willson Hour," a nice assertion of local pride, but at this late date we may as well speak frankly: in his pre–*Music Man* celebrity, Willson did Middle America more harm than good. He was the model of the genial wisecracking bandleader, a Doc Severinson of the Grape Nehi age, making the poison pill of TV and national radio go down easily in the heartland.

Yet in his comfortable exile, Willson dreamed Iowa. He wrote marches, croon-tunes, and even the "Iowa Fight Song" for his home state. And in the late 1950s, after years of gestation, he came forth with *The Music Man*, his wise, warm-hearted, funny, and enduring play about a con-man who falls in love with the Iowa townspeople he came to swindle.

The musical was an astonishing success, with a Broadway run of 1,375 performances. It has since become a staple of community and high school theater, which I say by way of praise, not disparagement. Willson's subject, after all, is community.

There is a wonderful photo of Meredith Willson at the 1958 North Iowa Band Festival, held in Mason City. The composer was fresh from his *Music Man* triumph; he had the world, and more importantly his home-town, in his pocket. As the Mason City High School band launched into "Seventy-Six Trombones," Willson leaped from his parade car, comman-deered a baton, and, to thunderous applause, led his alma mater's band in his signature composition. What a moment that must have been for a small-town boy. Unlike Curry, this prophet *was* with honor in his home-town.

If any American composer understood the Willsonian obsession with marching bands it was that New England original Charles Ives of Danbury, Connecticut, whose bookkeeper father was leader and chief cornetist of the Danbury Band and his town's "moving and controlling spirit in our musical matters."

Young Charlie idolized his dad and melded those grand passions of Middle America: by age fourteen he was a church organist, right halfback and captain of the Danbury Academy football team, and a wild-armed pitcher with a superb pickoff move.

He saw, with a kind of cranky Connecticut clarity, just where those media that bedazzled Willson were leading us. In his song "The Ruined River," Ives waxed threnodic:

> Down the river comes a noise!
> It is not the voice of rolling waters.
> It's only the sounds of man,
> Dancing halls and tamborine,
> Phonographs and gasoline.
> Human beings gone machine.

His biographer Jan Swafford writes, "As an adult, Ives detested radio, movies, and the other new media, seeing them as destroying the immediacy of contact between art and people." Town bands of the sort his father so proudly led would virtually disappear, replaced by "entertainment that only required the faceless, distant listener to turn a knob, and that horrified him." Or as the Southern agrarian Andrew Lytle said in his Ivesite apothegm: "Throw out the radio and take down the fiddle from the wall."

It was with the small-town democracy of Danbury in his mind and heart that in February 1920 Ives proposed, with a spectacular lack of success, his grand scheme for saving America: the Twentieth Amendment, a kind of national town meeting under which citizens—every single one—would propose national laws. Congress would select the ten most compelling proposals and submit them to a national referendum.

The amendment was Perot-like in its goodhearted and naïve impracticality. Ives would later support the Ludlow Amendment, that last gasp of populist isolationism which would have required a national referendum on a congressional declaration of war. In 1938, the composer wrote to the man who laid Ludlow low, President Roosevelt, deploring the bombing of civilians. In language that must be gibberish to the ears of CNN-watchers, Ives declared: "If a coward flies over and drops a bomb on a sleeping child's head, the only thing for a man to do is to rise up and get that dehumanized pigeon whether it brings us to war, hell, or Heaven."

Today that pigeon wears a chestful of medals.

If Ives's work was too dissonant for the Aaron Copland–Virgil Thomson school of Americanist composers, he was their spiritual kin, one of those New England eccentrics without whom our country is unthinkable. Paris, said Virgil Thomson in 1939, "has always reminded me of Kansas City." America reminded Charles Ives of Danbury.

And Cedar Rapids, to return once more to Iowa, reminded me of America defiled, scarified by the Interstate, soul-stolen by urban renewal. Grant Wood's wife, Sara, who comes off badly in most retellings of their short unhappy married life, sneeringly referred to "Cedar *Crick*" from her rarefied aerie of Iowa City. May the Crick rise again. (The superb Cedar Rapids Museum of Art, with its fine collection of Grant Wood and Marvin Cone, is a start.)

Cedar Rapids was once home base of Quaker Oats, the archetypal American company. How meet that the personification of the Middle American breakfast should be a Friend, by implication a pacifist, and that the wholesome foodstuff he represents should be a product of Grant Wood's city deep in the middle of irenic America. (The Quaker line included the other enduring image of the store-bought American breakfast, Aunt Jemima, though since Jesse Jackson's failed shakedown of Quaker in the 1970s the corpulent mammy has lost her bandanna and undergone a makeover into a kind of foxy pancake-flipping debutante. Hattie McDaniel melts into Halle Berry.)

I have the good fortune to know Robert D. Stuart Jr., the grandson of Quaker cofounder Robert Stuart. Mr. Stuart was the longtime CEO of Quaker, Reagan's ambassador to Norway, and the precocious organizer of the America First Committee in 1940–41, when he was a left-leaning midwesterner at Yale Law School who was convinced that the Second World War would be a replay of the First, a mad bloodfeast of carnage and conquest that the American Republic could not survive.

The first time I met Mr. Stuart I asked him if he, Gerry Ford, Potter Stewart, Jack Kennedy, Sargent Shriver, and the boys ever held America First reunions. "No," he smiled, "we did not. We may be a little sensitive to the fact that the world still thinks we're the bad guys." Peace, then and now, has been a lousy career move.

In the four years that I helped him with his memoir, I came to know Mr. Stuart as an exemplary man, loyal to his family, his ancestors, his home-town of Lake Forest, Illinois, and his country. If a levelling populist like myself could ever be won over to a benignant view of the American upper class, Mr. Stuart would be the instrument of my enlightenment.

In 2001, Quaker and its memorable trademark were swallowed by Pepsi—much to the disgust of old-time Quaker Oats people, Mr. Stuart among them. He fought the sale bitterly—no, that is the wrong word; he fought the sale out of love for a company that, to him, consisted not of stock options but of human beings, of Stuarts and friends, of the ghosts of all who had come before, from the earliest hullers of oats. But the board of directors, eminently practical men of business, sold out to Pepsi, an entity Stuart regarded as a corporate vulgarian, rotting both teeth and morals. It is but a matter of time before the Quaker Man is either shelved or made to look more like Brad Pitt. (Grant Wood, curiously, did no work for Quaker. Nor was he with young Bob Stuart in 1940. Wood refused an entreaty from the America First Committee to design a poster on its behalf. He was no pro-war interventionist, mind you—just a Roosevelt Democrat back when that party had a volant rural wing.)

Thirty miles southeast of the Quaker plant is the birthplace of our first Quaker president, Herbert Hoover, who, unlike our second Quaker,

Mr. Nixon, took his faith's precepts seriously enough to be the closest thing to a pacifist ever to occupy his office.

Hoover defies understanding: orphan, peace-monger, engineer; a devout believer in vast energy projects (including the dam that is his memorial); a deep-dyed planner who sought ways to harmonize American individualism with cooperative effort; and a political puzzle whom his fellow Iowan, the radical historian William Appleman Williams, found endlessly fascinating, not least for his enigmatic remark during the Depression: "What this country needs is a great poem. Something to lift people out of fear and selfishness."

That poem was not to come from the brush of his neighbor Grant Wood, however: in his cross engineer mood, Hoover disparaged Wood's masterpiece, *The Birthplace of Herbert Hoover, West Branch, Iowa*, as too prettified. (What is it about midwestern artists and their Republican presidents? Meredith Willson—and this boggles the mind—composed a march for Gerald Ford's Whip Inflation Now program.)

Hoover is impossible to pigeonhole. He understood the virtues of decentralism. He detested war and the preparation therefore and became a severe critic of the national security state. A weak-hitting shortstop, he knew that "next to religion, baseball has had a greater impact on our American way of life than any other institution."

What happens to our America when soccer rectangles replace baseball fields? Ask the Stepford Wife striding purposefully at the Million Moms March.

Alas, Herbert Hoover wound up living in the Waldorf-Astoria. It's awfully hard to see Iowa from there, no matter how large your window.

———————

Herbert Hoover, in his protracted dotage, would publish with the Henry Regnery Company, which during the 1940s and '50s released numerous volumes into the free zone that existed outside the de-Vitalizing Center.

The Henry Regnery whose name graced the publishing house provides an inspiring example of the fluidity of left and right in the 1930s, and the way that (oatless) Quakers enriched the weal.

Henry Regnery's father, William Henry, Iowa-bred son of German immigrants, was a Chicago textile manufacturer, vice chairman of the National Council for Prevention of War, and an almoner for peace. (He was the "largest financial backer" of the America First Committee, according to historian Wayne S. Cole.) Although he would come to despise Franklin D. Roosevelt after earlier supporting him, the socially concerned Regnery fit no stereotype of the avaricious businessman. He was a friend to Jane Addams and a director of Hull House; he also subsidized the experimental Quaker settlement of Penn-Craft, which is where his son Henry comes in.

In 1937, one of William Henry Regnery's friends procured for young Henry a summer job in the Resettlement Administration, where he got a firsthand look at the "bureaucratic nightmare" of the New Deal subsistence homesteads program. "I don't know that I accomplished anything," he told me with a grin when I interviewed him in 1996, "but I was impressed by government inefficiency."

He was favorably inclined to the idea of homesteading, however, and when Clarence Pickett, the "very superior man" who ran the American Friends Service Committee, asked Henry Regnery to assist the Quakers with Penn-Craft, a project in Western Pennsylvania, the Harvard graduate student agreed. After all, "it was about time I got out into the world and did something."

Soon after accepting the position with the Quakers, Henry met Eleanor Scattergood, who was also working for the American Friends Service Committee. In due time Miss Scattergood became Mrs. Regnery, and the couple embarked upon married life in the coal country of Fayette County, Pennsylvania.

Penn-Craft was built upon a 200-acre farm south of Pittsburgh. (The name honored William Penn as well as the Craft family, previous owners of the property.) Fifty unemployed coal miners and their families were resettled on this fertile land; most were of eastern European or old American stock. Each family was to live and grow food on two acres; another 100 acres were run as a commercial farm by an Indiana Quaker named David W. Day, who taught the colliers farming skills and sold them commodities priced as inexpensively as was practicable.

"It was entirely independent," said Mr. Regnery. "The Quakers were convinced that the failure of the government projects was because of the ineptitude of the government; if it could be done privately it would be successful."

A cooperative spirit suffused Penn-Craft, and the Regnerys were caught up in it. "Everybody helped everybody else," recalled Mrs. Regnery. "You spent some time helping your neighbor build his house, and he spent time helping you build yours." Temporary homes, later to house chickens, were quickly thrown up; a carpenter and mason then taught the homesteaders to build their permanent homes, which were constructed "of stone from the bee-hive coke ovens." ("They all finished their homes," Mrs. Regnery remembered, "and then instead of putting chickens in them, they rented them out!")

Clarence Pickett, in his autobiography *For More Than Bread*, summarized the optimistic atmosphere at Penn-Craft: "Here we had two hundred acres of beautiful farmland where, with the experience of government subsistence homesteads behind us, we and fifty homesteading families were free to work out to the best of our ability what we believed could be done by people with low incomes if they would only pool their labor and dreams."

But there remained the problem that bedeviled the New Deal homesteads: how to make peace with the cash economy. Enter Henry Regnery. His job was to establish "some sort of industry to provide employment and cash income."

"It sounded very easy," he said at a remove of almost sixty years, smiling at his youthful naïveté. Henry had just taken his Ph.D. examination at Harvard, where he studied with economist Joseph Schumpeter, but this confident young man presently discovered that his task "was far more difficult than it had appeared when I discussed it with Clarence Pickett in the comfortable surroundings of the Harvard Faculty Club."

Regnery's father encouraged his son to "learn something about business," and he did so, rather in the way that a boy thrown into a pond soon learns something about swimming. On Penn-Craft's grounds Henry "started a knitting mill which made cheap sweaters." The factory employed men as knitters and women to operate the sewing machines; the pay was twenty-five cents an hour, "and people literally fought for the jobs." Eventually the factory was churning out 200 dozen sweaters a week. But despite a workforce of "superior people, hard workers," Regnery's enterprise "never was able to make money."

After two years in the red, the Penn-Craft knitting mill was taken over by "a highly skilled knitting man from Vienna" who made a go of it. He made so much a go of it that he went, moving operations to Uniontown—"a rather ironical end," said Regnery, "to our attempt to establish a small industry for a homestead community."

Like other subsistence homesteads of the era, public and private, Penn-Craft fell victim, indirectly, to the Second World War. For the war machine was fueled, in part, by coal. Mrs. Regnery remarked, "As soon as the war came the men went back into the coal mines. They had more money, and they didn't want to work in the same way with the gardens; they didn't keep chickens." Those chickens, of course, would come home to roost— but not for a while.

The Regnerys cherished their two years at Penn-Craft. Their memories had a wistful, sometimes humorous air, for though the community was small and poor it rested on a foundation of mutual aid, hard work, and idealism. It contributed little to the GNP, it is true, but no community that brought together Henry and Eleanor Regnery, and set them on a marital journey that would last six decades, can ever be deemed a failure.

The Wapsipinicon River, which fed the riparian dreams of Grant Wood and Jay Sigmund, flowed through the farm in Troy Mills, Iowa, on which Bill Treichler grew up. His mother attended fifth grade with Grant Wood. Bill recalls that his father "used to say that Grant could really paint before he started the poster stuff."

Almost sixty years ago, Bill Treichler, newly discharged from involuntary service as a gunner on a Flying Fortress, entered a subscription to Ralph Borsodi's magazine the *Interpreter*. Bill and his family soon befriended Borsodi, the gentle prophet of decentralist living whom Grant Wood quoted in "Revolt Against the City," and in the years since the Treichlers have lived in such a manner as to make Henry Thoreau look like a lotus-eating sybarite and MTV guest VJ. The late Mildred Loomis, "grandmother of the counter-culture," praised the Treichlers as the peerless three-generation homestead family in her volume *Alternative Americas*.

Bill met Martha Rittenhouse at Black Mountain College, the legendary proto-Beat school in North Carolina, where John Cage's discordant anti-notes fought the air. Bill was there to study weaving ("a man at one of the decentralist conferences wearing a hand-woven wool suit had made a big impression on me") and biochemistry (to learn "the scientific basis for organic farming"). Martha, the beautiful daughter of a Church of the Brethren farm family in Maryland, was studying art and writing with, among others, the mad poet Charles Olson. Martha was "a Maryland 4-H All Star" who designed and sewed her own clothes, so her match with Bill was tailor-made.

Bill and Martha were married in 1950 and lived next to his parents outside Troy Mills in a house the young couple built from "salvaged bricks and native lumber." Their aim was self-sufficiency: they raised five children and "nearly all of the food" that they needed. They lived happily on the few hundred dollars a year they made selling their corn, beef, and flour. Bill milled the flour and ran a one-man sawmill. Martha and the elder Mrs. Treichler sewed what the young family wore; at night, the children listened as their parents read aloud from the works of Trollope and Walter Scott.

Then along came Bill's old employer, Uncle Sam, ever on the lookout for scenes of domestic tranquility to bust up. The Corps of Engineers planned to dam the Wapsipinicon River and, incidentally, flood the Treichler farm. The Wapsie is the lifesource of Iowa culture: Wood is buried along its banks, and its morning mists bewitched Sigmund, the poetical Cedar Rapids insurance executive.

It's just like the U.S. government to damn life along such a river, and though the dam never was built, the Treichlers moved on, spending the next several years farming and teaching at private schools in Colorado and Vermont until they had saved enough money to pay cash for eighty-seven acres of land in New York's sublime Finger Lakes region. The whole family renovated a decrepit, circa-1830 farmhouse that had domiciled more squirrels and skunks than a Beatrix Potter menagerie: from post to beam, their home outside Hammondsport is now a local treasure.

The Treichlers embody the best tradition of the American pioneers, and they do so without an ounce of sanctimony. Friendly and unpretentious, they wouldn't dream of condemning neighbors who enjoy a Big Mac. ("Be joyful though you have considered the facts," as Wendell Berry advises.) They are almost giddily optimistic, as they see more families returning to the land and doing things—including teaching their young—for themselves. "Families living in the country will come to be self-reliant," says Bill. "Parents are already doing better raising children. Homebirths and homeschooling will produce a generation of confident achievers."

No doubt there were oddballs aplenty in the pre-hippie American counterculture, ranging from nudists advocating land reform to hopelessly citified intellectuals going "back to the land" (without any clear idea of what to do once they got back) to Tolstoyan pacifists ready to fight at the drop of a name. But it included profoundly healthy people as well, and none more so than the Treichlers.

Though they can hardly be said to be followers, Bill and Martha read avidly the work of Ralph Borsodi. Borsodi's once-popular *Flight from the* City (1933) encouraged a going-out into the country, a rustication that would lead to a revival of home and domestic industries. Borsodi was no technophobe but rather among the first believers in what would later be known as "appropriate technology." He called "mass education" a "dreary waste of time" and stated that two hours of schoolwork were sufficient for a child: the rest of the day ought to be devoted to "reading and play," by which he did not mean Gameboy but rather "play . . . related to useful functions."

The Treichlers took from Borsodi what made sense and practiced it with love, joy, familial cooperation. Their lives are evidence that it *is* possible to live on a human scale amid the giantism of modern America.

And yet, though the tale of the Treichlers has a happy ending—the generations still gather for the weekly Saturday evening meal, not a take-out pizza but rather a feast to which each member of the family has contributed—it has not all been a sunny idyll of picking sun-kissed strawberries on a hill. I want to quote at length from a letter Bill Treichler wrote me in September 2004. For Bill's is, perhaps, the scolding voice of decentralism past—and perhaps decentralism future:

> You have more faith in midwesterners than I do. I used to believe that rural people were the real people who had all the right motives and values, but not anymore. I think the people who settled the midwest were plungers. They were plucky and they worked hard, but they believed in getting rich. They wanted to make it big . . .
>
> The plains ranchers overstocked the range and the small farmers there broke grassland to raise wheat. By the thirties a dustbowl was the result.
>
> From what I saw last spring, the farmland of Iowa and the other central states will be exhausted in 50 years at the rate they are cropping it now. If energy prices rise to make fertilizers uneconomic, yields will fall and commercial

agriculture [will] collapse. That has to come, but it will be tragic for those people. This country will no longer be a food exporter in competition with local farmers of many other lands. That will be good for those distant people and it will force more Americans to produce food for themselves, and that will be good for us because we will eat fresher more nutritious food and work to improve our gardens. The organic revolution was won some years ago. Who is not today convinced that they should avoid chemicals?

Although I am pessimistic for the near future I do think that many people, those who have moved to rural homesites, will learn to take care of themselves, their families, and be able to help their neighbors. The move to the country by individual families has been a spontaneous phenomenon. Few reporters seem to have noticed the new houses and the fixed-up places on rural acreages along nearly every road in this region [the Finger Lakes], and the side roads we traveled on our trip to Iowa last spring.

This has happened since . . . Ralph Borsodi and Mildred Loomis promoted decentralist living. Another great spontaneous movement, homeschooling, emerged after the decentralist period and continues to accelerate. It started with the people who didn't want their children to be taught evolution. Why should they be forced to send their children to schools that taught what they did not believe? But homeschooling has gone beyond the fundamentalists now. Religious beliefs won't really matter, children who are with their parents all the time and frequently with grandparents, aunts and uncles will grow into confident, capable and happy people.

Rural, basically self-sufficient, living, along with homeschooling and the interconnectedness of the information age, will produce people who will be more self-reliant and more insistent upon independence. And they will have the time and inclination to fashion beautiful, purposeful homes and gardens and tools, and to express their own ideas and feelings by writing, drawing, painting, speaking, singing and dancing.

Sunday we spent the whole day canning tomatoes. We did 74 quarts. We are picking up apples and some weekend soon George will get out his cider mill. Martha and I have been cutting up apples and freezing applesauce.

Thus speaketh Iowa.

Thus speaketh, out of the dim mists of our republican past, America. But is its voice intelligible to our imperial American ears? At some point in post–World War II America, the Middle West and all its Middle American manifestations became inexplicable. Take Donna Reed, without question the most beautifully American-looking actress of the Cold War era. Donna was an Iowa girl, a tomboy who grew up playing baseball with her brothers on the farm—watch her hurl that rock at the window of the old Granville place in *It's a Wonderful Life*; what a wonderful arm! She was an Iowa Republican who was for her fellow Iowan Henry Wallace in 1948, for Barry Goldwater in 1964 because the Kennedy-Johnson Democrats offended her Iowa isolationism, and for Eugene McCarthy in 1968 for the same reason. Viewed through old-fashioned American glasses, Reed's politics make perfect sense as the expression of a girl who attended the one-room schoolhouse in Nishnabotna, Iowa, and won a blue ribbon at the Iowa State Fair for the whole-wheat yeast rolls she made for the Nimble Fingers 4-H Club. It is only in the funhouse mirror of postwar American politics that the Donna Reeds are contorted and the Arnold Schwarzeneggers look normal. (William Appleman Williams of Atlantic, Iowa, the New Left historian who pined for a return to the Articles of Confederation and regarded Charles Lindbergh as the last and greatest

American hero, is perhaps the male version of Reed. Or would that be Grant Wood, dreaming of an American art arising from the Nishnabotnas, the Atlantics—far from the ocean—the Anamosas . . .)

For Donnabelle Mullenger to become Donna Reed she had to move to Los Angeles, which had become the capital of American cinema due to the coal shortages of the First World War, which had been fought over the futile objections of Iowa farmers.

It's the same old song, isn't?

> I fought L.A.
> And L.A. won

Or in the plangent trill of the Oscar Wilde of mope-rock, Morrissey of the late great Smiths:

> We look to Los Angeles for the language we use
> London is dead, London is dead, London is dead

So it seems on alternate days. But not always.

Just for fun, why don't we pretend that our culture is reclaimable. That it's not too late for America to tip Wood-ward, rather than for the Woods to be clearcut by Rupert Murdoch, the Disney Channel, and Starbucks.

Because even a whirlwind visit can hearten those who despair of a lockstep America. Sure, the outskirts of every small city in the country beg to be skirted, and the car radio in the age of Clear Channel seems to confirm Phil Ochs's lament, "I would be in exile now/ But everywhere's the same." But it's *not* the same. Not yet.

Miles Wolff, first commissioner of the reborn Northern League, which bucked the majors-minors system and brought independent professional baseball to the twenty-first-century Dakotas, said that the league's founding reminded him of *The Music Man*: "If they believe, it happens."

You can believe in the American Empire, with its smart bombs and dumb presidents, or you can believe in the American Main Street, where Sinclair Lewis and Grant Wood lived. You can believe in Clear Channel or you can believe in Clear Lake.

In 1939, after an Oxford education, the Iowa poet Paul Engle realized:

> *My life is*
> *To be at home here by the cornfield's edge,*
> *Under the big light of American sky*

The cornfields are still there—no immutable law of state or economy says that they can't be tilled and harvested by families. The sky is as big as ever—no space shuttle or projectile of the military-aeronautical complex can block even a millionth part of the empyrean. There is no reason why Iowa, why inner America, why even my Main Street can't once more strike up the band.

CHAPTER FOUR

Wendell Berry on War and Peace

Or, Port William Versus the Empire

*"I think the first thing that made me dislike imperialism was
the statement that the sun never sets on the British Empire.
What good is a country with no sunset?"*

—G. K. CHESTERTON

The first casualty of war is not truth—that expires during diplomacy—but the country.

Wendell Berry—exemplary countryman; man of place in a world run by the placeless; farmer, poet, agrarian, novelist, Kentuckian, essayist, and patriot whose world, fictive and real, is what localism looks like—has chronicled the ways in which war and the preparation therefore drain the countryside and feed the hypermobility that is the great undiagnosed sickness of our age.

War devastates the homefront as surely as it does the killing fields. Soldiers are conscripted, sent hither and yon to kill and maim or to be killed or maimed; their families relocate, following the jobs created by artificial wartime booms. War is the great scatterer, the merciless disperser. How you gonna keep 'em down on the farm when Mom and Pop and Sis have found Elysium in Detroit?

Nothing of nobility, perhaps even nothing of necessity, dignifies foreign wars in Berry's world. When, in *A Place on Earth*, Ernest Finley returns a cripple from the Great War in 1919, he finds his parents dead, their home sold. He is staggered by "the implausibility of the fact that something so vast as a war had picked out and defeated so small a thing as one man, himself." The sun also rises, but this doughboy does not.

The First World War, that maiden voyage of the U.S. military across the oceans to "make the world safe for democracy," in President Wilson's ringing phrase, is but an adumbration of the Second in Berry's fiction.

"It was 1916 and a new kind of world was in the making on the battlefields of France, but you could not have told it, standing on Cotman Ridge with that dazzling cloud lying over Goforth in the valley, and the woods and the ridgetops looking as clear and clean as Resurrection Morning," we read in the story "Watch with Me." A clan of eccentrics is Port William's first war casualty:

> There had been a time when a Proudfoot almost never worked alone. The Proudfoots were a big family of big people whose farms were scattered about in the Katy's Branch valley and on Cotman Ridge. They liked to work together and to be together. Often, even when a Proudfoot was at work on a job he could not be helped with, another Proudfoot would be sitting nearby to watch and talk. The First World War killed some of them and scattered others.

The childless Tol Proudfoot, last of his era, dies, appositely, in 1941. His world soon follows.

In Berry's fiction, the Second World War is the great climacteric. By 1942, says Hannah Coulter, "A great sorrow and a great fear had come into all the world, and the world was changing. I grew up, it seems to me, in the small old local world of places like Shagbark and Hargrave and Port William in their daily work and dreaming of themselves. . . . But then, against the fires and smokes of the war, the new war of the whole world, that old world looked small and lost. We were in the new world made by the new war. . . ."

Hannah marries her first husband, Virgil Feltner, "as war spread across the world." *A Place on Earth* (I quote from the 1983 revised edition) opens in that bleak first winter of the war, as fathers and uncles, including Mat Feltner, Virgil's father, play cards in Frank Lathrop's empty store, minified by "their sense of helplessness before an immeasurable fact." For what is there to do at home during war but wait and work, tormented by absence?

According to Croesus, "In peace the sons bury their fathers, but in war the fathers bury their sons." Mat is deprived of even the meager solace of such an interment. Virgil is reported missing in action at the Battle of the Bulge; he is never to return. As his wife explains in *Hannah Coulter*, Virgil would "disappear, just disappear, into a storm of hate and flying metal and fire. . . . Virgil was missing, and nobody ever found him or learned what happened to him."

Tom Coulter, whose grim job it is to bulldoze the anonymous dead into mass graves, precedes Virgil in death. As Hannah says, "One day we knew that Tom Coulter was dead somewhere in Italy. Nothing changed. There was no funeral, no place to send flowers or gather with the neighbors to offer your useless comfort."

Tom's brother Nathan, who will marry Hannah after the war, fights in but rarely speaks of the Battle of Okinawa, where, his wife surmises, the soldier "lived inescapably hour after hour, day after day, killing as you were bidden to do, suffering as you were bidden to do, dying as you were bidden to do." It is no life for a man, as Berry makes clear in "Manifesto: The Mad Farmer Liberation Front," wherein he counsels, "As soon as the generals and the politicos/ can predict the motions of your mind,/ lose it."

War, kens Hannah, "is the outer darkness beyond the reach of love, where people who do not know one another kill one another and there is weeping and gnashing of teeth, where nothing is allowed to be real enough to be spared." The reach of love, a frequent Berry trope, might extend to eastern Kentucky on a good day but never, ever, to Europe. Or even Washington.

The deaths overseas are not explicable; they are as senseless as the drowning of little Annie Crop in *A Place on Earth*. Nathan Coulter pithily describes the Battle of Okinawa as "Ignorant boys, killing each other." (This is not to say that Port William boils with antiwar anger. Old Jack Beechum carries around a newspaper picture of FDR, exhorting the president: "Go to it. By God, we're for you, sir." These are yellow-dog Democrats, even as their community is riven by a Democratic president's war.)

According to Hannah Coulter, "I think this is what Nathan learned from his time in the army and the war. He saw a lot of places, and he came home. I think he gave up the idea that there is a better place somewhere else. There is no 'better place' than this, not in this world."

It was a conviction never again shared by U.S. policymakers.

The instruments of American displacement in the last century have been various, but Berry quite rightly—and courageously—locates many of them in what has come to be known, especially among those who did not fight in it, as the "Good War."

Conscription was the least of these deracinating forces: after all, the draftee, if he was lucky enough to survive, came home. But to what did he return? To a land denuded by the great exodus of rural Southerners, black and white, to the industrial cities. More than 15 million Americans, or 12 percent of the civilian population, resided in a different county in March 1945 from the one they had resided in on December 7, 1941—and this doesn't even count the 12 million-plus who were wearing Uncle Sam's khaki.

The border states were especially hard-hit: as an anti-hillbilly joke of the 1940s went, America lost three states during the war: "Kentucky and Tennessee had gone to Indiana, and Indiana had gone to hell."

The diaspora of rural Southern blacks was no less tragic. Uprooted and urbanized blacks found otiose those skills that had been necessary to country life. Some were consumed by the vast industrial armies that, for a time, promised steady and remunerative employment; others fell into welfare. The verdant countryside of black farmers that might have been was eclipsed by urban moonscapes of sullen slum-dwellers. (In my home county of Genesee in New York, the Good War swept able-bodied farming men into the army or the factory, creating an absence in the fields that was filled by migrant workers: people from away, people who had no stake in the land, in the region.)

In Berry's fiction, the Second World War is a watershed in manifold ways: it rends, it depopulates, it mechanizes, it destroys. So do its offshoots.

Hannah Coulter refers to "the interstate highway that transformed everything within its reach." The people-scattering National Interstate and *Defense* (my italics) Highway System was conceived during World War II by top-down planner extraordinaire Rexford G. Tugwell and made concrete by an itinerant general named Dwight D. Eisenhower, who had admired Hitler's autobahn and got one of his own.

Tugwell, chief ideologist of the New Deal, had defined the American farm as "an area of vicious, ill-tempered soil with a not very good house, inadequate barns, makeshift machinery, happenstance stock, tired, overworked men and women—and all the pests and bucolic plagues that nature has evolved . . . a place where ugly, brooding monotony, that haunts by day and night, unseats the mind." To Tugwell and the highwaymen, the Interstate over which the benighted peasantry might relocate to a Cincinnati suburb was no mere ribbon of road: it was a lifeline.

Since those who write books and make movies and TV shows are distinguished as a class by their mobility, we seldom get an honest reckoning of the cost of modern nomadism. If anything it is celebrated as the flowering of the human spirit.

Nor do we often assess the domestic effects of militarism, or should I say militarism's effect on domesticity. The cost of war might be measured not only in body bags, in returning boys without legs, arms, eyes, faces, but also in divorce, dislocation, novels never written, children not fathered. During the Second World War, the divorce rate more than doubled, normal patterns of courtship were disrupted, Daylight Saving Time was imposed nationwide over the objections of rural America, and the subsidized daycare industry was born via the Lanham Act, which sponsored 3,000 daycare centers to incarcerate the neglected children of Rosie the Riveter. (To be fair, the war did prove a boon to the moving and storage industry.)

The Second World War, says Hannah Coulter, changed the ideal "descent of parcels," which is "for every farm to be inherited by a child who grew up on it, and who then would live on it and farm it and care well for it in preparation for the next inheritor." Hannah's three children would leave home, forfeit their membership; this forfeiture is told in some of the most heartbreaking prose Berry has written.

This was by no means a generational fracture limited to the rural South; John P. Marquand, in his novel of the WWII homefront *So Little Time* (1943), calculated a similar domestic cost in the Northeast: "There was no use thinking any longer that someone who belonged to you might live in your house after you were through with it."

Burley Coulter, in Berry's story "The Wild Birds," expresses it this way: "I thought things would go on here always the way they had been. The old ones would die when their time came, and the young ones would learn and come on . . . And then, about the end of the last war, I reckon, I seen it go wayward. Probably it had been wayward all along. But it got more wayward then, and I seen it then. They began to go and not come back . . . the young ones dead in wars or killed in damned automobiles, or gone off to college and made too smart ever to come back."

But the place to which they did not return was not the place they had left. "[T]he days before the war were 'the old days,' sure enough," admits Hannah Coulter. "The war changed the world. The days when Nathan and I were little, before we had electricity and plumbing and tractors and blacktopped roads and nuclear bombs"—all the conveniences of the modern world—were perhaps beyond reclamation.

"There was no TV then," she recalls, which is to say that vital regional cultures might exist. But then almost every healthy manifestation of local culture was smothered—terminated—strangled—by U.S. entry into the Second World War. The Iowa poetry renaissance. The efflorescence of Upstate New York fiction. The regional theater movement. Hell, even North Dakota cornhusking contests. (Don't believe me? See Gordon L. Iseminger, "North Dakota's Cornhusking Contests, 1939–1941," *Agricultural History*, Winter 1997.)

War nationalizes culture; it exerts a centripetal force that shreds what it does not suck in. A Cold War would follow, logically, the abandonment of traditional American neutrality in the two world wars; its policy fruits, besides the aforementioned Interstate, included the acceleration of school consolidation, a profoundly anti-community movement conceived by progressives of the Big is Beautiful stripe that was given wings by the militarism of those allegedly halcyon 1950s, when the chimera of well-drilled little Ivan Sputnik was used to regiment the comparatively anarchic American educational system. Schools were centralized, which eliminated local idiosyncrasy, local accents, removed parents from the daily life of the schools, and finally led to the virtual nationalization of the curriculum. Consolidation made war upon the school as a repository of shared memory, as a physical manifestation of community culture. No Coulter girl would ever again be graduated as valedictorian from Port William High School. For there was no place for Port William High in the "changed world."

Yet a homeplace remains central to any possibility of a good life. In "Making it Home," a story from *Fidelity*, Berry describes one of the lucky ones—a revenant. A soldier who has his place to which he can return.

After three years as an expendable cog in a military machine, Art Rowanberry, a member of Port William, returns—alive. Art travels homeward by bus as far as Jefferson—a town name pregnant with meaning. He hoofs it the rest of the way, as the fetters of the myrmidon fall off, for "whatever was military in his walk was an overlay, like the uniform."

Over there, Art was unmoored, "trusting somebody else to know where he was," marching without aim or knowledge of his surroundings. Walking home, he is now separated from his place, his anchorage, by "only a few creeks that he knew by name."

Art Rowanberry "had been a man long before he had been a soldier, and a farmer long before he had been a man." The armed services had no use for farmers and little more for men. "From a man used to doing and thinking for himself, he became a man who did what he was told."

Appraising the "fine brick farmhouses" by the roadside, Art muses that the illusion of their permanence had been shattered by the army: "We wouldn't let one of them stand long in our way."

"Farms, houses, whole towns—things that people had made well and cared for a long time—you made nothing of."

Coming home from killing, from "the unending, unrelenting great noise and tumult" of death and the slaughter of strangers, from "little deaths that belonged to people one by one," Art is once more made whole by his gradual reabsorption into his Kentucky ground.

"Making it Home" is rich in the language of incompleteness: "We blew them apart and scattered the pieces so they couldn't be put back together again." Art sees his war as "the great tearing apart," after which "nothing was whole," and of course the same is true, in its way, of the homefront the men left behind. War blows communities apart, scatters the pieces, and even Port William would not be put together again, not really.

Taking his leave of Uncle Sam, Art is the cussed independent, the "insubordinate American" in which Robert Frost placed his trust: "The government don't owe me, and I don't owe it. Except, I reckon, when I have something again that it wants, then I reckon I will owe it."

That due bill would come a generation later, when the government drafted the sons of Art Rowanberry's generation for a war that no one in power even bothered to declare.

Of Art, Berry writes, "It pleased him to think that the government owed him nothing, and that he needed nothing from it, and he was on his own. But the government seemed to think that it owed him praise. It wanted to speak of what he and the others had done as heroic and glorious. Now that the war was coming to an end, the government wanted to speak of their glorious victories."

Art Rowanberry, it appears, would never fall for any of the Greatest Generation hokum of a half-century later. One doubts his acquaintance with the Collected Works of Tom Brokaw's Ghost Writer.

"They talk about victory as if they know all them dead boys was glad to die. The dead boys ain't never been asked how glad they was," observes the veteran. Nor were the dead boys consulted beforehand. The Department of War requested their presence; they complied.

Having been separated from home, Art, like so many of his coevals, might well have been cut adrift forever, dying slowly of inanition brought on by residence in the WildeWood Lanes of suburbia or on the nineteenth hole of Myrtle Beach. For a melancholy moment he is struck listless with "aimlessness, as if, all his ties cut, he might go right on past his home river and on and on, anywhere at all in the world." But he presses homeward, taking refuge and nourishment in an empty church, and in the bright morning "[h]e was in his own country now, and he did not see anything around him that he did not know."

He will come upon his father and brother and nephew plowing, and if a fatted calf is not repast at the reunion, nonetheless his father rejoices, prodigally, telling Art's nephew, "Honey, run yonder to the house. Tell your granny to set on another plate. For we have our own that was gone and has come again."

———

Sounding like the old Populists, Art Rowanberry notices that "[t]he government was made up of people who thought about fighting, not of those who did it." The division is no less stark today: Set up an arm-wrestling tournament and I'll guarantee you that Johnny Mathis could pin pretty much every *National Review–Weekly Standard* talking-head bombardier.

The rootless send the rooted to die. But it was not until the next generation of young men marched off to war that the people who did the fighting would, in any appreciable numbers, stand up and say No.

Since the Spanish-American War, the South, despite its status as a conquered province, has been much the most hawkish region of the country. The Georgia populist senator Tom Watson might ask of the Spanish-American War, "What do the people get out of this war? The fighting and the taxes." But southerners fought for the Union in 1898 with all the dash and bellicosity with which their grandfathers had fought to sunder it in 1862.

They were, in the main, every bit as hawkish in the twentieth century's two world wars. Diplomatic historian Wayne S. Cole notes that "in no section of the nation did the America First Committee encounter such uninterrupted, vehement, and effective opposition as it met in the South." The subsequent war might decimate their country, but southerners as a whole supported it with a fervor rivalled only in New York City.

The pattern of southern (and border-state) enthusiasm for war was maintained during Vietnam, cooked up by the graduate-degree-stamped products of the northeastern ruling class but fought in disproportionate number by denizens of hollows and hamlets never dreamt of by McGeorge Bundy.

When Wendell Berry delivered "A Statement Against the War in Vietnam" on February 10, 1968, to the Kentucky Conference on the War and Draft, he adverted to the ambient martial mood:

"I am a Kentuckian by birth, by predilection, and by choice. There are a good many people in this state whom I love deeply. And of all those perhaps only four believe that I should be speaking here today—and one of them is me."

Berry speaks only briefly to the particular case of Vietnam, finding it an Orwellian entanglement. "We seek to preserve peace by fighting a war, or to advance freedom by subsidizing dictatorships, or to 'win the hearts and minds of the people' by poisoning their crops and burning their villages and confining them in concentration camps; we seek to uphold the 'truth' of our cause with lies, or to answer conscientious dissent with threats and slurs and intimidations." He asks where in the Gospels, the

Declaration of Independence, or the Constitution the leaders of our ostensibly Christian and democratic nation find authorization for such actions.

But Vietnam, while perhaps an especially unlovely canker on the body politic, is only a sympton of "a deadly illness of mankind": that unholy melange of selfishness, violence, placelessness, and greed against which Berry has tilted his lance these forty years.

In this speech, Berry reveals himself to be a pacifist, or very nearly so. "I have come to the realization that I can no longer imagine a war that I would believe to be either useful or necessary," he says. Due in part to the technological enhancement of the weaponry of war, its unimaginably vast potential for slaughter, "I would be against any war." (Except, one suspects, a war to repel an armed invasion of Kentucky.)

He recognizes war's collateral damage: the curtailed civil liberties, the despoiling of the land and its bounty, the hypertrophied bureaucracy, the erosion of national character that is inevitable as we "become a militarist society" with "a vested interest in war." He denies "absolutely the notion that a man may best serve his country by serving in the army": the uniform that Art Rowanberry wore a generation earlier connotes, certainly in 1968, servility, not service.

But Berry's preponderant reason for opposing war—any war, not just Vietnam—is located in the innermost of those concentric rings of citizenship: his family.

> As a father, I must look at my son, and I must ask if there is anything I possess—any right, any piece of property, any comfort, any joy—that I would ask *him* to die to permit *me* to keep. I must ask if I believe that it would be meaningful—after his mother and I have loved each other and begotten him and loved him—for him to die in a lump with a number hanging around his neck. I must ask if his life would have come to meaning or nobility or any usefulness if he should

sit—with his human hands and head and eyes—in the cockpit of a bomber, dealing out pain and grief and death to people unknown to him. And my answer to all these questions is one that I must attempt to live by: *No.*

Berry says much the same thing in his Cold War–era poem "To a Siberian Woodsman":

> *There is no government so worthy as your son who fishes*
> *with you in silence beside the forest pool.*
> *There is no national glory so comely as your daughter*
> *whose hands have learned a music and go their own way on*
> *the keys.*
> *There is no national glory so comely as my daughter who*
> *dances and sings and is the brightness of my house.*
> *There is no government so worthy as my son who laughs,*
> *as he comes up the path from the river in the evening,*
> *for joy.*

Berry descants on this theme in "Some Thoughts on Citizenship and Conscience in Honor of Don Pratt," an essay inspired by a University of Kentucky student who would spend two years in federal prison for refusing induction into the U.S. Army—or, in the invidious phrase of the day, dodging the draft. (Berry would elsewhere propose raising the draft age from 18 to 40, a deadly serious piece of whimsy earlier suggested by William Jennings Bryan, among other antiwar populists.)

"My devotion thins as it widens," explains Berry. "I care more for my household than for the town of Port Royal, more for the town of Port Royal than for the County of Henry, more for the County of Henry than for the State of Kentucky, more for the State of Kentucky than for the United States of America. But I *do not* care more for the United States of America than for the world."

This last sentence divides Berry from the antiwar isolationists, with whom he otherwise has much in common on matters of foreign policy. Like them, he abhors militarism and foreign wars; unlike them, he sees peaceable potential in cooperative international agreements. Wendell Berry is no nationalist:

> *I sit in the shade of the trees of the land I was born*
> *in.*
> *As they are native I am native, and I hold to this place*
> *as carefully as they hold to it.*
> *I do not see the national flag flying from the staff of*
> *the sycamore,*
> *or any decree of the government written on the leaves of*
> *the walnut,*
> *nor has the elm bowed before monuments or sworn the oath*
> *of allegiance.*
> *They have not declared to whom they stand in*
> *welcome.*

Berry shares the spirit of the great literary anarchists of the American tradition: Thoreau, Edward Abbey, William Saroyan, even Edmund Wilson. He sounds Concordian notes in his Pratt essay, lamenting that "the state is deified, and men are its worshippers, obeying as compulsively and blindly as ants." He desires neither alms nor arms from the state, averring that "the government cannot serve freedom except negatively—'by the alacrity,' in Thoreau's phrase, 'with which it [gets] out of the way.'"

Still in the Thoreauvian vein, he asserts: "I wish to testify that in my best moments I am not aware of the existence of the government. Though I respect and feel myself dignified by the principles of the Declaration and the Constitution, I do not remember a day when the thought of the government made me happy, and I never think of it without the wish that it might become wiser and truer and smaller than it is."

This is Wendell Berry the rural anarchist, the reactionary radical, the lover of his country and contemner of its government. As he adjures in "Manifesto: The Mad Farmer Liberation Front":

> *Denounce the government and embrace*
> *the flag. Hope to live in that free*
> *republic for which it stands.*

If he is usually assigned to the left pen of our hopelessly inadequate and painfully constrictive political corral, that is because by the 1960s conservatives had largely renounced peace and stewardship—once cornerstones of a broad movement capacious enough to include Senator Robert Taft and the authors of *I'll Take My Stand*—and embraced finance capitalism, development *uber alles*, and an interventionist foreign policy.

"The great moral tasks of honesty and peace and neighborliness and brotherhood and the care of the earth have been left to be taken up on the streets by the 'alienated' youth of the 1960s and 1970s," writes Berry in *The Hidden Wound* (1970). If he aligned himself—provisionally, with many stated reservations—with the Left, it was because the Right objurgated peacemakers as unpatriotic. Yet Berry understood the New Left, or at least the spirit thereof, as an essentially "conservative" movement, as we were told at the time by sources ranging from Paul Goodman to SDS President Carl Oglesby to *Easy Rider*. (Goodman—a New Yorker, a Jew, a promiscuous homosexual, and a self-described "conservative anarchist"—located the modern derangement in "TV, mass higher schooling, the complex of cars, roads, and suburbanization, mass air travel, the complex of plantations, chain grocers, and forced urbanization; not to speak of the meteoric rise of the military industries and the Vietnam war and the draft." He insisted that there was nothing "inevitable" about these catastrophes: they were the result of conscious policies, pursued by rational men in the service of progress.)

Wendell Berry in the 1960s marched under no banners, stood for nothing larger (or smaller) than what he stood on. His touchstone was not Karl Marx or Herbert Marcuse but Thomas Jefferson, the political figure most often quoted by Berry in essays and poems. Like Jefferson, the polymathic planter "with his aristocratic head set on a plebeian frame," in Vernon Parrington's phrase, he insisted that "[t]he small landholders are the most precious part of a state." Like Jefferson, who opined that "our General Government may be reduced to a very simple organization and a very inexpensive one, a few plain duties to be performed by a few servants," Berry scorned the massive state. And like Jefferson, he is an anachronism in post-republic America. Among the tragedies of contemporary politics is that Wendell Berry, as a man of place, has no place in a national political discussion that is framed by Gannett and Clear Channel.

Apropos Don Pratt, Berry wonders whether he ought to feel "great shame in going free while good men are in jail because of their goodness." Thoreau, after all, did his time, hard as it wasn't. But Henry David was a bachelor, dependent-less as he was independent, while Berry is a husband, a father, a farmer, and these blessings entail obligations which a political prisoner cannot fulfill. Again, Berry's boy trumps politics, the state, the outer—the more distant—world.

These remote and impersonal institutions are undeserving of loyalty anyway. It is simply not possible to pledge allegiance in any meaningful way to an entity as large and abstract as the nation-state.

"My country 'tis of the drying pools along Camp Branch I sing," Berry hymns in the poem "Independence Day." His country is that which is within the range of his love, his understanding: not a bloodless (if bloodthirsty) abstraction at the other end of a TV tube but rather the dirt of his backyard. In the acronymical argot of our day this praiseworthy sentiment, this love and active cherishing of home, is derided as selfishness, as NIMBY—Not in My Backyard—by those who have no backyards.

Yet it is only in defense of one's backyard that a "cause" achieves justness. Without "land under us/ to steady us when we stood," a political movement, even one so putatively well-intentioned as the anti–Vietnam War coalition, is doomed to a formless rage that is as ugly, in its way, as the McNamara-Rumsfeld cold calculus of death. As Berry writes in "A Standing Ground":

> *uprooted, I have been furious without an aim.*

Behold the anger of the deracinated, who know what they hate but not what they love—whose motivation *is* hatred, never love. Berry warns that the peace movement must not "become merely negative, an instrument of protest rather than hope." He cautions, prophetically as it turns out, against "self-righteousness and disillusionment and anger."

The life of the professional protester, the chronic placard-carrier and slogan-shouter, is desiccated and desolate. "The political activist *sacrifices* himself to politics," Berry writes in "Some Thoughts on Citizenship and Conscience in Honor of Don Pratt"; "though he has a cause, he has no life.... Unsubstantiated in his own living, his motives grow hollow, puffed out with the blatant air of oratory."

The wandering activist of the '60s was every bit as placeless as Richard M. Nixon. Credit-card-carrying members of the "nation of transients" could not credibly protest the war because they rested their case upon the defense of . . . nothing. To combat nomadism, one must make a home; to combat violence, one must embrace peace, and that peace is more, much more, than the mere absence of war.

Berry was never one of those inveterate petition-signers and microphone-hoggers, the frenetic engaged intellectual ever attaching himself to Worthy Causes Which No Person of Intelligence and Goodwill Can Gainsay.

> *I am not bound for any public place,*
> *but for ground of my own*

Like charity, dissent begins at home—*with* a home.

Homeways lies renewal. Berry ends his essay on Don Pratt and war by proposing not a change in administrations, not a get-out-the-vote drive or a March on Washington, but rather the reclamation of rural places, a restoration of the class of "independent small landowners," à la Jefferson. Such a move would, he envisages, "restore neglected and impoverished lands, and at the same time reduce the crowdedness of the cities. They would not live in abject dependence on institutions and corporations, hence could function as a corrective to the subservient and dependent mentality developing among government people and in the mass life of the cities."

Though the etiology of the maladies be remote, the cure is at hand. As Berry poetizes in "February 2, 1968":

> *In the dark of the moon, in flying snow, in the dead of*
> *winter,*
> *war spreading, families dying, the world in danger,*
> *I walk the rocky hillside, sowing clover.*

It sure beats napalm.

———

There was about Vietnam a whiff of missionary liberalism, at least at first, as Kennedy's best and brightest sought to reproduce the Great Society in Southeast Asia, in Hubert Humphrey's hubristic threat. The idealistic among the war hawks were consumed by the "gleeful imperialism of self-righteousness," to use a Berry term, not unlike those church missions that always travel to remote and allegedly benighted climes, so much more exotic than the shantytown down the road. The Lord seems to call an awful lot of Christian missionaries to Kazakhstan and Bolivia but precious few to the trailer park on the edge of town.

A kindred Marine-borne uplift virus is detectable in President George W. Bush's campaign to "rid the world of evil," starting in Mesopotamia. For reasons both quintessentially American and unmistakably his own, Berry is out of sympathy with Bush's neo-Wilsonian plan to rescue the world for democratic global capitalism—whether the world wants rescue or not.

In "A Citizen's Response to 'The National Security Strategy of the United States of America,'" Berry finds in the Bush strategy, with its assertion of the right to preemptive attacks, "a radical revision of the political character of our nation." The executive is now the supereminent branch of a national state that grows more secretive and expensive, for the "war on terrorism" is "endlessly costly and endlessly supportive of a thriving bureaucracy."

In his 2003 essay "The Failure of War," Berry wonders "to what extent the cost even of a successful war of national defense—in life, money, material goods, health, and (inevitably) freedom—may amount to a national defeat." Randolph Bourne's aphorism has become an unassailable truism: War is the health of the state. As Berry writes, "Militarization in defense of freedom reduces the freedom of the defenders. There is a fundamental inconsistency between war and freedom."

Once more, Berry, as a patriot of his place, assays the domestic consequences of a foreign conflict. How will this war change life as it is lived in one's home place? (Not "homeland," an un-American locution foreign to our vernacular and which, prior to the ascendency of George W. Bush's speechwriters, was redolent of jackboots and hammers and sickles.)

Because Berry—unlike the makers of policy and manufacturers of punditry—has a home, he is trenchant and refreshing on the "homeland security" con: "Increasingly, Americans—including, notoriously, their politicians—are not *from* anywhere. And so they have in this 'homeland,' which their government now seeks to make secure on their behalf, no home *place* that they are strongly moved to know or love or use well or protect."

The root cause of the new U.S. imperialism is, as it were, the lack of roots.

Wendell Berry is no world-saver. He admonishes "You easy lovers and forgivers of mankind," those lovers of disembodied Men but despisers of particular specimens of the race, that

> *My love must be discriminate*
> *or fail to bear its weight*

Loving all equally, the humanitarian universalist loves none especially. He will raze a village in order to save it, jail the opposition in order to preserve freedom, and order boys from Port William into combat and death to prove with what value he endows all human life. (For his part, Berry nominates Dorothy Day as the most likely "planet-saver": that is, "a person willing to go down and down into the daunting, humbling, almost hopeless local presence of the problem—to face the great problem one small life at a time.")

The architects and archons of Empire, of the subordination of Port William to the needs of what Clinton's Secretary of State Madeline Albright so memorably called "the indispensable nation," fit Berry's description of the "'upwardly 'mobile' transients" who wage war upon our places: "They must have no local allegiances; they must not have a local point of view. In order to be able to desecrate, endanger, or destroy a *place*, after all, one must be able to leave it and to forget it. One must never think of any place as one's home; one must never think of any place as anyone else's home. One must believe that no place is as valuable as what it might be changed into or as what might be taken out of it. Unlike a life at home, which makes ever more particular and precious the places and creatures of this world, the careerist's life generalizes the world, reducing its abundant and comely diversity to 'raw material.'"

The arsenal of epithets that the publicists of the War Party use against their opponents is revealing: provincial, parochial, isolationist. For the most honest and compelling antiwar impulse comes from the love of the particular. In cherishing Port William or its real-life counterpart, Port Royal, one disdains to bomb Baghdad.

If Wendell Berry is not quite pacifist enough to suit the precisian—one has little doubt that he would use force to deter the mad rapist-killer of so many philosophical challenges hurled at the pacific—he will not countenance acts of war by the nation-state. He asks in "The Failure of War": "How many deaths of other people's children by bombing or starvation are we willing to accept in order that we may be free, affluent, and (supposedly) at peace? To that question I answer pretty quickly: *None.* And I know that I am not the only one who would give that answer: Please. No children. Don't kill any children for *my* benefit."

Once more we espy the Siberian woodsman. The "enemy"—who has never done or even contemplated doing the least bit of harm to Port Royal—has a face. His children live in Novosibirsk, Baghdad, Hiroshima, Hanoi, Teheran . . . even Atlanta.

Once there was a way to get back home. Art Rowanberry found it. We can, too. Hannah Coulter tells it better than anyone:

> We all know what that beautiful shore is. It is Port William
> with all its loved ones come home alive.

But is that way back home still open? Is it in any sense "the American Way"?

Staying at home, after all, is for losers. I recall an academic (Roy L. Brooks by name) writing in the *New York Times* that Supreme Court nominee David Souter was manifestly unqualified for the position by virtue of residing "in a tiny New Hampshire town" and living "in the same small farmhouse in which he was born."

High crimes in the *Times*! Souter's attachment to his place was refreshing, no matter what one might say of his subsequent work on the Court. But our rulers and those who articulate their prejudices saw it as heretical hermitage.

Or consider the courtier historian Richard Hofstadter, whose noxious *Paranoid Style in American Politics* (1966) is hauled out every time a journalist (who has never read the book) wishes to explain why some madmen might be dissatisfied with a choice between, say, John Kerry and George W. Bush. Hofstadter wrote of the Great Commoner, "Intellectually, [William Jennings] Bryan was a boy who never left home." Just what this means is murky enough; presumably it condemns Bryan's refusal to sell out his neighbors on the Plains and sign up with J. P. Morgan or Herbert Croly.

Far better, in the eyes of Hofstadter and Roy L. Brooks, to be Archibald Higbie in Edgar Lee Masters's *Spoon River Anthology*:

> *There was no culture, you know, in Spoon River,*
> *And I burned with shame and held my peace.*
> *And what could I do, all covered over*
> *And weighted down with western soil,*
> *Except aspire, and pray for another*
> *Birth in the world, with all of Spoon River*
> *Rooted out of my soul?*

Higbie, we may be sure, voted for Woodrow Wilson, read the *New Republic*, and hadn't a trace of either paranoia or attachment to his native ground.

Archibald Higbie would be nonplussed by Wendell Berry's declaration that "a man must be judged by how willingly and meaningfully he can be present where he is, by how fully he can make himself at home in his part of the world." Hofstadter would find such sentiments jejune. But some of us understand.

For despite Horace Greeley's famous injunction to abandon one's home for a vagabond's fortune out West, the unmythicized Americans have always chosen to stay, not stray. The irresponsible may push on, pulling up roots and westering, pushing on toward the sunset, leaving soil erosion and deforestation and sobbing mothers in their wake, but the stay-at-homes have understood the link between an "enduring agriculture and an enduring society," as Steven Stoll wrote in his fruitful *Larding the Lean Earth: Soil and Society in Nineteenth-Century America* (2002).

One man's American Dream is another's tragic diaspora. The political implications of restorative agriculture have been "conservative" in the authentic sense of that much-abused word: rooted, home-centered, mindful of the holiness of small things. Vermont Whig Rep. George Perkins Marsh, extolled today as a father of American environmentalism, "tried to make the case that people who become native to their place do not leave it," as Stoll writes. Marsh also was among the most eloquent critics of the Mexican War on the charming grounds that the U.S. was quite large enough, thank you. (Marsh can hardly be claimed as an ancestor by the Big Green environmentalist organizations. His faithful localism was poles apart from the old-money Eastern Republicans who asserted federal hegemony over vast stretches of a West that they knew mostly through picture postcards or the cowboys-and-Indians vacations of rich boys.)

The careless have always been the first to pick up and move—a coward's game, no matter what the mythmakers tell us. As romantic as prairie schooners and the Hesperian exodus to the fruited plain may be, the real honor resides with those who stayed put. They were not timid souls, afraid of a challenge, but the real heroes of the settling of America.

One of them lives in Kentucky.

CHAPTER FIVE

A Working-Class Hero Is Something to Be

Carolyn Chute and Other Insubordinate Americans

> "Many of my intellectual generation sold out. First to the
> Communists, then to the organized system, so that there are
> very few independents around that a young man can accept as
> a hero."
>
> —PAUL GOODMAN

Carolyn Chute's return address includes the postscript "No Fax/
No Phone/No Paved Road." The self-taught novelist of Maine's
backwoods can add "No More Good Reviews," for in the late
1990s she did the unthinkable in post-McVeigh—not to mention post-
9/11—America: she founded the 2nd Maine Militia and agitated for revolution. Carolyn calls the 2nd Maine "the militia of love," and while she is
dead serious, her career is seriously dead.

In June 1999 we came to Carolyn Chute's Parsonfield, Maine, from
Concord, Massachusetts, where Gretel plunked imaginary redcoats on the
rude bridge that arched the flood. (Two hundred-plus years ago, New
England had use of militiamen.) We were borne, not on the night wind of
the past, but on the ribboned highways of the present. The McDonald's
we passed in Westbrook was selling a Lobster Value Meal—who says
there's no place for regional cuisine under global capitalism?—but not for
nothing has Maine been relegated to the far corner of the country: Un-
grateful vandals keep throwing rocks through the window of the Starbucks
in Portland.

The German and Swedish cars that hum along the Maine coast give way, the further inland one goes, to pickups, until our green Lumina starts to look suspiciously hoity-toity. Carolyn's hand-drawn map, with such landmarks as "Big old place" and "old trees," is a cartographic masterpiece, as for once we make no wrong turns.

We find her dirt road near the Maine–New Hampshire border. She has posted a speed limit of 3.5 miles per hour on the rutted path that leads to the wooden frame home, set amid the seventeen hilly wooded acres that the 1985 best-seller *The Beans of Egypt, Maine*, bought for Carolyn and her husband, Michael.

Michael greets us at the door, standing at attention, cradling a reproduction Brown Bess. He is artillery commander of the Border Mountain Militia; Gretel thrills to the sight of this Revolutionary War ghost. Lucine snaps photos of Gretel assuming martial poses before various militia flags. I half expect to see them used as evidence at our Thought Crimes trial.

Michael has a ZZ Top–quality beard and a soft Maine drawl. He mows and tends the town's gravesites, filled with the bones of his ancestors and relatives. His people have been here since 1830; "this town is all related to him," says Carolyn. Michael is eight years younger than Carolyn, but she calls him "Pa." She first saw him at a turkey shoot in Sebago. He cannot read, so she reads her work aloud to him. This is natural: "Home is work in common," Carolyn says. "Home is life in common." (Such a union, however, is uncommon: Name another American novelist whose spouse is illiterate.)

There exists a dreary sub-genre of regional writing by displaced professors who move to college towns and see the hirsute and saggy locals lolloping along Main Street and crank out novels in which they imagine the squalid lives of loutish husbands and victimized wives and feral children, one of whom may score well on the SATs and escape Boggy Creek for the faculty lounge. Carolyn Chute is not one of those. She is the real thing: a Maine girl who married a Maine boy and would no more betray Maine than she would turn over her guns to the Proper Authorities.

Carolyn is an inveterate scrawler and sign-maker. Tables and walls and the refrigerator are blazoned with such messages as "School Stinks" and "Neo-Isolationist and Proud of It." Draped over the Stars and Stripes is the Border Mountain Militia flag, designed by Carolyn and bearing the image of the Abominable Hairy Patriot. ("The Indians believed that in terrible times, a big hairy guy would come and warn the people.") The Chutes have a thing for hybrid creatures: Michael's drawings of dogmen (half man, half man's best friend) are eerie and ubiquitous. Purebreeds are at home here, too; we sit in the chairs usually occupied by the Chutes' Scottish terriers.

Carolyn rocks steadily, laughs readily. She tells us that she was raised in Cape Elizabeth, on the coast, before "the professional people came in and it got built up." She uses "professional people" as a pejorative, for the invaders inevitably corrupt "what I like about small towns: You had a relationship." "Even the person in town you don't get along with, you hate, you always wave to him," interjects Michael. "You might be stuck in a snowbank sometime, and he'll pull you out."

No one is going to pull Carolyn out of the critical hole that *Snow Man*, her fourth novel, dug her. Since our visit in 1999 she has been buried under enough scorn and obloquy to suffocate a weaker woman. And all because she loves her neighbors and her country.

Snow Man follows Robert Drummond, a hairy and occasionally abominable patriot, a Maine militiaman who is between assassinations, as it were. He has just executed one U.S. senator from Massachusetts and would be drawing a bead on the other were it not for the gunshot wound to his shoulder administered by Boston police. Robert is taken in by a sympathetic handyman on the estate of his intended second target, Sen. Jerry Creighton, who is known as "the Liberal, which means he works *hard* for the rights of blacks and gays and women and foreigners who have graduated from Harvard . . . or Yale . . . and he works hard for the rights of Big Business, as does the rest of Congress."

Robert will be nursed, in ways medical and otherwise, by

Creighton's daughter, an "angry, rivalrous ultrafeminist," and his Beacon Hill wife. The novel is about "what happens when the 'left' and the 'right' come together, heart to heart," writes Chute, who dedicates it to, among others, Noam Chomsky and the 2nd Maine and Border Mountain Militias.

Chute opens *Snow Man* with a brief scene so jarring that you half expect the novel to be interrupted while the author is issued a citation for having a Hate Thought. In a Boston barroom decidedly not that presided over by Ted Danson, cheers go up as the first senator's assassination is reported on TV. "Get 'em all!" is the general sentiment, though one patron cautions the celebrants to "Watch out. I heard of a guy who was arrested and put away for saying that kinda thing. An' he was just a poor old retarded guy almost eighty years old."

"This is America. I speak my mind," replies one bold toper. To which Chute appends, "In barroooms and living rooms and dooryards and workplaces all over America, people discuss the senator's demise, followed by awkward discussions of the dangers of speaking one's mind." It is a lesson that Carolyn Chute, theretofore a critics' darling, has learned with a vengeance.

"With all my other books I got jillions of interviews," she says. But with *Snow Man*, "they won't interview me. And I don't think it's that much more poorly written." The folks at Harcourt Brace tell her it's "controversial," to which she replies, "It can't be controversial if it's blacked out!"

Snow Man's assumption that militias are indigenous expressions of hearty patriotism perhaps kept Michiko Kakutani and Garry Wills from embracing the novel. But Chute's disparagement of corporate-ladder feminism is what really seemed to irk reviewers. The flunky in the *New York Times* singled out the passage in which Drummond explodes, "the big-boy fucker in the White House and his arrogant bitch broad femmie-Ms. wifey"—remember, this is 1999—"and the banker boys eat my Constitution for breakfast and tell me I can't have a gun because I might fuckin' use it."

We are not in Bobbie Ann Mason country.

"Liberals hate working-class white men, especially those who don't do dishes and who whistle at women," wrote Chute in an essay rejected by the *Nation* in the wake of the Littleton, Colorado, school shootings. (Never mind that the dynamite duo were spoiled suburban brats, the rotten products of military families and consolidated schools.) Carolyn Chute loves working-class men, and she believes this forbidden love is one reason the worms of the critical world turned on her. Feminist reviewers "don't like bedroom scenes when women are having a nice time. They want them to be beaten in the head, then finally escape at the end from brutal guys. [Robert's] not brutal, he's just . . . a guy. He's sweet." Though the dead senator might demur.

Outlets that routinely praise books featuring every sort of depravity, from self-mutilation to the cerebrations of Francis Fukuyama, took after *Snow Man*, whose adultery scenes might aggravate the Legion of Decency but hardly qualify as "pornographic," as *Publishers Weekly* had it. (PW also found the book "alarming in tone.")

My theory of why reviewers hated *Snow Man* is this: In Chute's previous novels, her Beans and LeTourneaus kept to their own trailers, their own hamlets. In *Snow Man*, one of Chute's hairy Maine men has escaped—and he's in *their* neighborhood, waving a gun, messing with their women!

Snow Man is filled with angrily sardonic observations on the chasm that separates corporate women from their working-class sisters. When Robert rues that his wife, Cindy, had to get a job to pay his mother's nursing home bills—the Drummonds "couldn't take care of her anymore. Too busy chasin' the dollar"—the senator's wife replies, "Well, that's wonderful. . . . A woman needs a career as much as a man does."

Robert explains that as a housewife, Cindy had been a canner and gardener and knitter and photographer and baker and blueberry picker; as a career gal, she was a slatherer of ketchup on strangers' Quarter-Pounders at McDonald's. Excellent discipline for a budding cog in the global economy, but who wants to ride the fast track to servitude?

Chute has worked for even lower wages than a McDonald's hand—she was a charwoman and potato-picker before *The Beans of Egypt, Maine*, her first and best-selling novel—but it is the grey-flannel blouse jobs that she most despises. The "establishment feminists," she tells me, "think we should all be head of a corporation or Ann Richards [D-TX]—the killingest governor—that's where women belong. *Nobody belongs there!*"

Chute signalled a turn toward the political when she dedicated her third novel, *Merry Men* (1994), not only to farmers ("America's last vestiges of freedom") but also, less conventionally, to "all those millions who were born to be farmers, as they have been for thousands of years, but because of modern 'education,' Big Business, and Mechanization they cannot be and will never know their true gift but are instead herded into welfare lines, prisons, or the slavery of Big Business."

This is the plight of her people, and it has driven her to a rural radicalism that is as American as Shays' Rebellion. "Is it really virtuous to lie down in peace when your people are being assaulted, heart, body, and soul?" asks the senator's comprehending wife in *Snow Man*.

Is assassination—murder—really the answer? "Oppression is not nice," Carolyn replies. "Revolution is not nice. But revolution is a reflex to oppression." Yet there is, as Dorothy Day lived and learned, a better response to oppression. Carolyn knows. For in the end, she writes of Love, of the would-be murderer whose hand is stilled by "that suffusion of empathy which some call God, some call weakness." She closes *Snow Man* with Geronimo's chilling plaint: "I think I am a good man, but . . . all over the world they say I am a bad man."

"That applied not only to Robert but also to the senators," she explains. "Many of us think of them as bad people. They're not—the system makes monsters out of people."

Chute need not look far for a genuine expression of dirt-road patriotic resistance to that system: for she is the founder and indefatigable secretary of the 2nd Maine Militia (450 members at its peak) and a stalwart of the smaller, localized Border Mountain Militia.

If a rat deserts a sinking ship, what do we call those brave souls who climb aboard and start bailing? Carolyn launched the 2nd Maine after the Oklahoma City bombing, when "it started to look bad for militias. I wanted to give them a good name. I thought this was really cool, there was a lot of potential, and I wanna make sure this doesn't die. Don't hide. They're all shy, these were the people who sat in the corner in school. Get out and be proud, fly your flag."

So Carolyn and an activist from the leftist Labor Party organized the 2nd Maine Militia. Their early meetings were a true rainbow coalition. There were "guys in camo, hippies, bikers, old ladies, Republicans, Democrats, Greens, Marxists, Libertarians, John Birchers. It was so cute!" says Carolyn with delight.

What do they have in common? "They're all trying to make sense of this. You talk to them, and they all sound sort of similar: The only thing that seems different is the information they're getting." Much of that information now comes from Carolyn, who as secretary fills the mailboxes of her comrades with articles from the *Nation*, *Shooting Times*, and other publications ranging from mainstream to the sort of *samizdat* that would hurl Alberto Gonzales into a tizzy.

Among the 2nd Maine's first projects was a raid on the Maine statehouse. One hundred and fifty militia men and women converged in Augusta. "We're screaming, 'We the People! We the People!'" recalls Carolyn. "It was so cool."

Alas, a few EarthFirst! monkeywrenchers showed up and taped a sign reading "Augusta: Capital of Corporate Terrorism" over the portrait of former Governor and Union Army hero Joshua Chamberlain, thus scotching any chance of being idealized in a Ken Burns documentary.

The 2nd Maine got a bit too big for Carolyn's taste. "My idea was have it be tribal: Different people start their own militias all over the place and then we get together to do a big thing. . . . People can develop their own style, their own neighborhood. People don't want large organizations—they won't go, especially the country people don't wanna sit under fluorescent lights and eat healthy snacks and raise money for petition drives."

Even in militias, she found, the articulate—"the professional class— would dominate. The conservative [which she uses as a synonym for work- ing-class] guys want to come and shoot their guns and while they shoot they talk. They stop, they talk, they shoot: They're doing something. If they get a moment where they don't want to talk they shoot. It's not like they're sitting there staring at each other waiting to have this . . . *thing*."

The 2nd Maine and Border Mountain Militias, please note, are nothing like the yokelish death squads that haunt the condominium dreams of Morris Dees and Hollywood scenarists. To Michael and Carolyn Chute, "the militia of love" marries the rural gun and shooting culture with the best of the do-your-own-thing hippie ethos. It proclaims itself "no-wing," for as Carolyn writes, "It is my deepest wish that the left, right, and all in between stop pointing horizontally when they say 'enemy' but look up at that faceless elite."

No-wing militias "are not right-wing and we are not Socialists. . . . [W]e do not want Centralized Power of any kind. We do not want a GIANT THING that industrializes people or treats them as a mass. We like having a BIG Constitution. But more local economies, regional, flex- ible, human."

The Chutes are not theocrats or racial separatists. The spring we met in Maine, Michael and Carolyn were organizing a multi-militia gath- ering to protest the drug war, no-knock searches, and the "undeclared martial law being practiced on our urban brothers and sisters." She dreams of a coalition between rural whites and urban blacks: After all, the drug war has filled the prisons with the latter, and an eventual gun-control war would introduce farm boys to this emerging growth industry.

"The government is going to try to take away our guns," Carolyn predicts, and "[a]ll of us naughty INDEPENDENT Yankees will thumb our noses at this. So now we'll be prime prison material. . . . I personally promise that if someone comes to bother me about my guns, I SHALL bite 'em in the ankle and rip off at least one ear and curse their tribe for twenty and one centuries."

Gun control hits all her buttons; it opens her Chute, you might say (if only her name were not pronounced "Choot"), as placeless yuppies and the regime they serve seek to strip rural people of a traditional American right. Michael and Carolyn have lived with guns all their lives. She remembers, "My sixth-grade teacher used to let the kids bring their hunting rifles to school and lean them against the wall. My husband bought a really good shotgun from a kid in the hall at Sacopee Valley High. I used to carry a huge hunting knife and unopened pack of cigarettes in my pocketbook. I never intended to use either one, but I'm the kind of gal who if you tell me I shouldn't do a thing, I shall do it (unless it is a cruel thing). If I were a young kid in high school today, I would have an unsmoked joint and a gun in my purse, because you tell me I can't. I would be searched, then handed over to the police."

It is among Carolyn's greatest insights that the conflict between "the professional people" and the natives in Maine mirrors that between indigenous people and rich outsiders elsewhere in the world. The rootless consumers masquerading as the left in America get misty-eyed over foreign peasants fighting the big landowners and multinationals, but they hate and fear the American working class and peasantry, especially when Jethro has a gun. Part of this owes to the upper-middle-class upbringing of the Java lefty: Everything he knows about life in the wilds outside Scarsdale he learned on TV; viz., that people who never went to college are ponytailed wife-beaters who lynch uppity blacks. The old missionary impulse is also at work: Rigoberta Menchu is so much more tinglingly exotic than Robert Drummond.

To the mobile professional, the gun has become the symbol of the immobile redneck. It must be confiscated; he must be emasculated. "Yuppies moving into our town post their land, holler for more police and want everyone to mow their grass and spruce up to their tastes and you guessed it . . . no more gunfire," writes Carolyn.

Her novels are about tribal loyalties; Chute is an encomiast of village life. Her politics, and those of her militias, are largely an outgrowth of
this faith.

"We don't see how dangerous the loss of small town life is," Chute
insists: "small biz, interdependence, the front porch, aunts and uncles who
live next door, Grammies who live next door. We call these losses progress,
or just a little trade-off for 'success.' NOBODY IS HOME! NOBODY IS
EVEN IN TOWN!"

Yet "[i]n our blood and bones we remember real mothers, real fathers, real aunts and unks. We remember protection. Security. We remember being stroked, fondled, cherished, being the future of our tribes. We
remember (more recently) friendly cops. Some of us remember before TV
when the living room chairs faced each other. Further back, we remember
the front porch. We remember when singing and stories were free. . . . And
yuh, those songs and stories were about us and our families, our personal
histories, in which our parents and unks and aunts were featured in heroic
ways."

Our job, she writes, is to recreate "a country made of thousands of
small healthy & various communities + tribes." This will not be done at
the point of a gun. "We do not plan to shoot ANYBODY," she scrawls in a
militia recruiting poster. "We want everyone safe and happy. *Everyone.* Our
guns are not for starting trouble. We only protect. We are not an Imperialist army. That is what the USA government military is for."

Her militia do not propose to end corporate privilege through
Naderite regulation; rather, they demand, in best Jefferson-Jackson fashion, the revocation of corporate charters and a law that "no one person or
corporation can own more than one newspaper or magazine." This may
run afoul of the First Amendment, though change that to "TV or radio
station" and now we're talking. But still, given that it is the bottom of the
ninth and the home team is trailing by several dozen runs—maybe the
game was over sixty years ago, but there are some things we are better off
not knowing—desperate times call forth radical solutions. As these Loco

Foco measures would effectively dismantle Microsoft, Disney, the *New York Times*, and Gannett, they will become "issues" when CNN covers the death of a 68-year-old diabetic janitor who loved his family but never dated Charlize Theron.

At the end of *Merry Men*, Chute introduces a lady preacher, a Casy for the laid-off millworkers of Southern Maine, who gives a succinct formulation of the Chute program:

> Our only hope ... is interdependence. We need to start saying "no" to jobs with big business and their products ... whenever there's a choice. We need to rely on each other. We need to support each other ... whatever's left of your small businesses and farms, your tradesmen. To hell with buying American. Buy or trade with your *neighbor*! Buy from that *face* not the brand name! Do this whenever there's a choice, even when it costs a little more. What price can we put on our freedom?
>
> ... For thousands of years we grew our own food. In two or three generations those skills have been stripped from us. Schooling has done this. And we condoned it ... this reverence for the white shirt, the desk, the clean hands, the books, the computers, the bucks, the conveniences, the "good job" somewhere else! How many survival skills do your children have? How many kids today can provide for themselves food, tools, clothing, warmth ...? Please, please, please, in the *name of God*, pass along any skills you have ... any of the old skills ... teach ... your sons and daughters ... whisper your secrets to your neighbor's child!

The teaching will not be done in the schools, according to Carolyn, for the purpose of education is the creation of the Professional. When, in *Snow Man*, the senator's wife asserts that "education" is the key to solving every problem under the sun, Robert retorts, "don't gimme that shit about education fixin' this. We don't wanna be yuppies. We can't *stand* the sight of yuppies. The only education we want is to find out what the hell's really goin' on."

Robert's son "has a computer that the school pestered the parents to get. Some deal with a big company through the school. Since the computer arrived, Josh never does anything with Robert, never even looks at his father, because his face is always stuck in his computer."

Carolyn believes the school is the enemy of the family. It is cold and vast. "Look at a small town," she says. "How cozy people are. We look after each other—even those we don't like. 'He's one of ours.' New York City is big and impersonal—why would we take a school and turn it into New York City and think that's an improvement?"

Michael adds, "They don't teach faah-min." (Pardon this lone lapse into dialectal transcription—the Chutes' accents are so natural, so unaffected, so unlike the popsicle-stick-on-tongue "aaaah" of the cartoon New Englander.) "How to live off the land—they don't teach those skills. They look down on faah-min."

"If you can get people skill-less, they have to work in your mill," says Carolyn, who fingers the industrial revolution as the culprit. "Spend the whole day in school with a pen and paper whether you can do that kind of thing or not. We have all these people who can't do anything who would have been farmers. They'd be surviving. They can't anymore. They're living in slums, in trailer parks."

"*They* send a yellow bus to our doors and we gladly shove our children aboard. For many years, day in and day out, the Great Society whispers into each sweet perfect little childly ear. . . . The Great Society begins at five years old. And notice how schools in no way resemble home. There are no grammies or dads, babies or dogs hanging around to lend or need a hand."

Her sympathies are with the quiet boy in the back of the room, the mousy girl who gets straight C's. Her imagination is rural, which is to say she understands how *right* it is for farmboys to trade shotguns in the halls, or girls to skip class to catch polliwogs. "Schools are treacherous places to us old Yankees," she says.

Her solution? "We need to blow up the schools and throw all the TVs into Boston Harbor. We do not want anybody in the schools when we blow them up. In fact, it would be rather nice if 80 percent of the population supported the effort. A great circle of people all holding hands will surround each brick fluorescent-lit school building. Songs of liberty will be sung. Flags will be waved. A cute 99-year-old retired schoolteacher will toss the first stick of dynamite."

That is classic Chute: insurrection with a heart, revolution with wit. The militia of love.

And hey, she may be right about schools, and she's certainly right about TV. No less than Edith Wharton deplored the "atrophying" of the "ghost-instinct" by "those two world-wide enemies of the imagination, the wireless and the cinema." I like to think of Edith and Carolyn, two lady novelists, lighting the fuse that will blow the idiot box back to the hell whence it came.

Carolyn realizes that her bridge to the land of well-fed sheep, of the *New Yorker* and the grant pasture, is forever burned. Twenty years ago, she was hailed as one of the freshest voices in American fiction. *The Beans of Egypt, Maine* sold 350,000 copies. By 1999, she was imagining an interviewer asking, "Are you going to give up writing if no one buys your books anymore?" To which she replied, "I will slowly starve and I will get very thin and weak and the power company will shut off my lights and I'll get weaker and weaker and weaker and die with a pencil in my hand in the dark. Unless I go to jail for having unregistered guns. There they will feed me and provide lights. But no pencil."

Carolyn was "feather-dusting" her next novel, the epic *The School on Heart's Content Road*. It was to be her *Grapes of Wrath*. But it never appeared. Perhaps it never will. Carolyn has not published since *Snow Man*. She may never publish again. For is a blackout ever lifted? "Once you're gone, you can't come back," as a ragged fellow sang, though if Carolyn were willing to rat on her friends and write books justifying her perfidy she might eventually win the Elia Kazan Prize at the National Book Awards. But old Yankees do not squeal.

She keeps writing. She stays in Maine. She ran a "low-budget" (practically no-budget) write-in campaign for governor in 2002. "Remember," she told voters, "it is Carolyn with a 'Y' as in YEOMAN and CHUTE with a hard 'CH' as in CHICKADEE." In a letter to me in April 2005, she expanded her platform to include "4 new laws. Against the law to wear a watch. And no more turn signal lights on vehicles. Only hand *signals*. No more road widening. And . . . everybody must wave to everybody." Carolyn, you are too good to be governor. Somewhere, Grant Wood, with his homemade finger turn-signal, is nodding.

Carolyn is not alone. She has ancestors, you know; aye, she has kin far and wide, throughout reactionary radicaldom.

Carolyn Chute views daycare, compulsory education, "establishment feminism," and most of the bedrock of the modern American professional's existence as inimical to healthy family and community life. In this she is like her antecedent, the labor radical and anti-feminist Mother Jones, a classic reactionary radical who was, to use Norman Mailer's lapidary self-description, to the left of the liberals and to the right of the conservatives.

Today we know Mother Jones primarily as the name of a magazine for consumerist liberals whose idea of a radical act is selling their R.J. Reynolds stock and buying Starbucks. The real Mother Jones—Irish-born Mary Harris Jones (1830–1930), the coal miners' angel and raiser of holy hell who said "I would fight God Almighty himself if he didn't play square with me"—was to her namesake magazine as Thomas Jefferson is to *The Jeffersons*.

Her nickname was not bestowed sarcastically. Mother Jones, whose husband and four young children had died of yellow fever, venerated the family as she did the strike. She hated the rich not least because they hired others to care for their children: "The rich woman who has a maid to raise her child can't expect to get the right viewpoint of life," she wrote in *Miners Magazine*. "If they would raise their own babies, their hearts would open and their feelings would become human. And the effect on the child is just as bad. A nurse can't give her mother's love to somebody else's child."

Mother Jones detested the middle-class reformers who sought to transfer household functions to the market or the state. She suspected that capitalists were scheming to force women into the paid labor force and children into daycare, and the prospect did not please her: "The human being is the only animal which is neglected in its babyhood. The brute mother suckles and preserves her young at the cost of her own life, if need be. The human mother hires another, poorer woman for the job."

(Her suspicions had foundation. As the family scholar Allan C. Carlson has noted, the National Association of Manufacturers was the most powerful lobbying force behind the ushering of women into the industrial workplace. The NAM was widely believed to have subsidized the National Woman's Party, fountainhead of the Equal Rights Amendment and lair of the noxious Alice Paul, who demanded that "the State assume entire responsibility for the maintenance and education of children." Yes, those were her words. Paul, who might easily have issued from the pages of a dystopian novel, has been latterly lionized in the pages of those social studies texts from which Mother Jones is conspicuously absent.)

Mother Jones was not given to conciliatory speech. She told striking steelworkers in Gary, Indiana, "I'll be 90 years old the first of May, but by God if I have to, I'll take 90 guns and shoot hell out of 'em. . . . We'll give Gary, Morgan, and the gang of bloodsuckers a free pass to heaven or hell."

The wives of the bloodsuckers were also the enemy: "The plutocrats have organized their women. They keep them busy with suffrage and prohibition and charity"—nuisance causes for upper-middle-class busybodies. As for Mother, "I don't belong to the women's club," she snarled. "I belong to the fighting army of the working class."

Like "Red Emma" Goldman, Mother Jones opposed woman suffrage. Goldman, however, was an Anti out of what some call misogyny and others call realism. "Woman, essentially a purist, is naturally bigoted and relentless in her effort to make others as good as she thinks they ought to be," argued Goldman. "Woman's narrow and purist attitude toward life makes her a greater danger to liberty wherever she has political power." Mother Jones, on the other hand, viewed suffrage as undermining the family. "Women are out of place in political work," she said in 1913. "There is already a great responsibility upon women's shoulders—that of rearing rising generations. . . . Home training of the child should be her task, and it is the most beautiful of tasks. Solve the industrial problem and the men will earn enough so that women can remain home and learn it."

A healthy family life was essential to Jones's individualistic American socialism. (I mean "individualistic" in a political, not social sense, as opposed to paternalist collectivism.) "Let the women stay at home and we shall have, when strikes come, better strikers," she said.

Arrogant lady reformers always drove her up a wall; Mother Jones would have enjoyed the anti-Mugwump song of the late nineteenth century:

> Oh, we are the salt of the earth,
> and the pick of the people, too;
> We're all of us men of worth,
> and vastly better than you.

The women of worth who bedewed themselves in toiling for the measly vote disgusted Mother Jones. "I have never had a vote and I have raised hell all over this country!" she protested. "You don't need a vote to raise hell! You need convictions and a voice!" (You still do: Carolyn Chute does vote—for Ralph Nader in 2004—but she also decorates her ballot with such protests as "If Voting really changed anything, it would be illegal.")

Contrast Jones with the termagants of the National Organization for Women, who stroked Senator Clinton's randy husband as though they were silky hookers. Mother Jones once met with President Taft to ask that labor radicals be pardoned. "Now, Mother," said Taft, whom she rather liked, "the trouble lies here: if I put the pardoning power in your hands there would be no one left in the jails."

To which she answered, "I'm not so sure of that, Mr. President. A lot of those who are in would be out, but a lot of those who are out would be in."

That is speaking Truth to Power.

Mother Jones, the working-class reactionary radical, is a non-person to today's feminist establishment, which insists that women occupy the same soul-draining jobs as men and takes it as a sign of progress that the harridanish likes of Hillary Rodham Clinton vote for spending, bureaucracy, and empire as rotely as do the men politicians.

In New York, Senator Clinton runs with the cross-endorsement of the innocuously named Working Families Party, but its platform is better suited to Rending Families, as Clinton's most cogent critic, the late Christopher Lasch, understood. In my brief and ill-starred graduate school career I was blessed to take a seminar with Lasch as he was writing his magnum opus, *The True and Only Heaven* (1991), among the most devastating debunkings of the god of Progress ever written.

The one-time Marxist Lasch had jumped the ideological track in the 1970s, "when my study of the family led me to question the left's program of sexual liberation, careers for women, and professional child care." From his youthful Henry Wallace–midwestern leftism, Lasch had come to a profound respect for the petit bourgeoisie, the small shopkeeper, and the rooted working class, who seemed always to be fending off, or losing ground to, the middle-class professional, the child-raising expert, the degreed social worker—those who know best how the unlettered ought to order their lives. By the 1980s Lasch was calling himself a "populist," attracted by neither political party, repelled by Reaganism and Clintonism alike. He was what a Family Left might look like, if such a Left were left.

The Nebraskan Lasch, the Yankee Chute, the Illinoisian Mother Jones, remind us of an age when the left, or that part of the left growing in the fecund soil of inner America, was as American as baseball, paperboys, and the Cardiff Giant.

Once upon a time, before the American small town had been reduced to a quaint prop in beer and truck commercials, its residents possessed a common understanding and sympathy so strong as to overcome such minor differences as those that separate Chute from patrician, lefty from righty, even president of the United States from leader of the Socialist Party.

The Socialist, in this case, was Eugene V. Debs, the radical Railway Union leader from Terre Haute, Indiana. The story of his release from prison has long tantalized me as a glimpse of the better America that was. That might be.

In Nick Salvatore's perceptive biography, Debs is presented first and foremost as a citizen of what the Socialist called his "beloved little community of Terre Haute, where all were neighbors and all friends."

"The Eugene Debs who achieved national fame as a strike leader and Socialist spokesman remained most profoundly a native son, born and raised in a small Indiana city," writes Salvatore. He had seen the relatively classless Terre Haute of his youth, his "enchanting little village," destroyed by industrialism, as the maple trees fell to the "hideous steel prison walls" of the modern factory and office building.

War hastened this grotesque transmogrification. Debs understood this, and for that understanding he was awarded the metal of honor. In June 1918, Debs told a Canton, Ohio, audience, "The master class has always declared the wars; the subject class has always fought the battles." After noting wryly that "it is extremely dangerous to exercise the constitutional right of free speech in a country fighting to make democracy safe in the world," Debs defiantly proclaimed, "I would a thousand times rather be a free soul in jail than to be a sycophant and coward in the streets."

He got his wish. Convicted of violating Woodrow Wilson's Espionage and Sedition Acts, Eugene V. Debs became the most celebrated of the 15,000 Americans whom even Wilson called "political prisoners." Debs was confined to the federal prison at Atlanta; in 1920, he ran for president from his cell and won almost one million votes, many from decidedly bourgeois non-socialists who admired his courage. H. L. Mencken, after mocking Debs for "his naïve belief in the Marxian rumble-bumble," praised him as "fair, polite, independent, brave, honest and a gentleman."

President Wilson, a Princeton intellectual, was vindictive in the manner typical of the theory class. "This man was a traitor to his country and he will never be pardoned during my administration," Wilson said of Debs. Chimed in the *New York Times:* "He is where he belongs. He should stay there." When Attorney General A. Mitchell Palmer, architect of Wilson's infamous Red Scare (it usually has been the liberals who persecute Reds), recommended a postwar pardon for the aged and ill Debs on Lincoln's birthday, Wilson's response was to scrawl a petulant "Denied" across the paper.

Wilson's successor was Warren Harding, the amiable owner of the *Marion* (Ohio) *Star.* Harding lacked Wilson's intellect as well as his mean streak. The kindly Buckeye asked his venial attorney general Harry Daugherty to meet with Debs in March 1921, so the prisoner was shipped northward on a train to Washington, where he met with Daugherty and Harding gofer Jess Smith. These Doublemint twins of GOP corruption were charmed by Debs. Although Daugherty opposed a pardon, he pronounced the Socialist "sincere, gentle, and tender," and the solicitous Smith even ran into a drugstore to buy a bundle of quill toothpicks for Debs after the prisoner complained of jailhouse plaque.

Among those pleading Debs's case was his Socialist Party heir, Norman Thomas, who by extraordinary coincidence had once been a dollar-a-week paperboy delivering Harding's *Star.* Thomas, who regarded the president as a genial Babbitt, "a fine small-town or city booster," visited Harding twice in the White House. The homeboys reminisced about good old Marion before Thomas asked, "Is it not a splendid thing that a country should have men brave enough to speak their minds even when they are in a minority?"

Harding agreed.

He intended to release Debs on July 4, but the American Legion protested so vociferously that he delayed the pardon from the anniversary of American liberty to the season of Christian charity. Harding released Debs on Christmas Eve 1921, saying, "I want him to eat his Christmas dinner with his wife."

The labor leader prepared to go home—not to a Washington, D.C., castle built upon union dues but to his pretty house in Terre Haute. At President Harding's request, Debs dropped by the White House on December 26. When the radical was ushered into the president's office, Harding sprang from his chair, stuck out his hand, and said, "Well, I have heard so damned much about you, Mr. Debs, that now I am very glad to meet you personally."

They chatted warmly, comfortably, in the way that a man who is esteemed in Marion can get on with a man who is esteemed in Terre Haute. Sinclair Lewis could have written it up, without the Rotary slang. In an oddly Middle American way, the pair had known each other all their lives. Debs later told reporters: "Mr. Harding appears to me to be a kind gentleman, one whom I believe possesses humane impulses. We understand each other perfectly. As for the White House—well, gentlemen, my personal preference is to live privately as an humble citizen in my cottage at Terre Haute."

And so the two Americans parted, the Socialist and the Republican, in perfect understanding.

I have ever loved this vignette for a number of reasons, not least that it suggests an age when America writ large still had certain of the qualities of a small town. I have seen the same fraternal and sororal comprehension extend throughout my hometown of Batavia; 'tis a wretch indeed who is a Republican or Democrat before he is a Batavian.

Henry Clay Owen, the "staunch Republican" editor of the *Terre Haute Post*, endorsed his "neighbor and friend" Eugene Debs for president in 1920, as his grandson Kent Owen told me. 'Twas a noble act of which the Owen family remains justifiably proud. Debs and Henry Clay Owen both were "gentle, generous, resolute," as Kent Owen says; they were honorable men, defenders of their town against the impersonal forces that would seek to drag low the Haute. What matter such trivial labels as Socialist and Republican when Indiana is at stake?

Debs, Chute & Jones—my kind of lawless firm—raise the questions that organized labor is too ponderously overorganized to ask. For instance: Why work?

Several years ago, San Franciscans rang in Labor Day, that drab and grey and pointless Monday that punches out summer as remorselessly as a time clock, with a "Rock Against Work" concert. A punk band caterwauled; speaker Bob Black demanded that we "commute the sentences of everyone sentenced to commute."

Most of the concert-goers marched off to work the next morning, but an important question had been asked: Why should wage labor dominate our lives?

How many of us partake of the quotidian pleasures that give our lives meaning—tossing a football with a child, reading to her, walking hand-in-hand with a spouse down the street where we live—but do so absentmindedly, blankly, all the while worried about the boss, the backlog, the impossible-to-please client? How many of us are wishing the years away, dreaming of retirement—only to wake up one morn, elderly and frail, and wonder where in hell the years went? "It goes so fast. We don't have time to look at one another," says Emily in Thornton Wilder's *Our Town*. And whose fault is that?

Some effects of overwork are obvious: stress, high blood pressure, nervousness. Others, though more subtle, are perhaps even more pernicious. For the first time in American history, a substantial number of children are being raised by someone other than their mothers. Some of these cases are unavoidable, and tots in the care of a grandmother or aunt or perhaps even next-door neighbor will probably be just fine.

But what of the children in institutional care: those who, à la *Brave New World*, are sentenced to daycare—State Conditioning Centres in Huxley's world—at a tender age? In many cases the parents live far from those family members or friends who might otherwise watch over the child—a remoteness that is, usually, the consequence of work. We move great distances for a few extra bucks, but is the speedboat or high-definition television really worth the loneliness?

Is that second full-time income really necessary? I drew an icy stare when in 1997 I posed that question to former Tennessee governor Lamar Alexander, then a presidential aspirant, now a senator. Alexander had made his pile of cash as vice chairman of Corporate Family Solutions, Inc., which operated ninety-five "child-development centers" providing daycare for the children of employees of Boeing and other Fortune 500 companies. I asked the Republican Alexander if "the pervasiveness of dual-earner couples" is "something that we should deplore." He conceded that "it's better for the mother . . . to be at home in the earlier months." Whereupon I asked:

ME: Months or years?

ALEXANDER: The earliest months make the greatest difference. But today, we have 75 percent of women who work away from home.

ME: Yeah, but many of those are part-time. A woman who puts her five-month old in all-day daycare: this is negligent, isn't it?

ALEXANDER: No, it's not negligent, not unless you want to say that millions of women are negligent. Of all the options available in that real-life situation, worksite care is best because it helps a working parent remain as attached as possible to a child. It's the same kind of help that a babysitter at home would be: women working at home don't spend every single moment with their child. The workplace becomes a new American neighborhood, in a sense, where you provide the kind of support that neighbors have traditionally given in the care of children.

Mother Jones or Lamar Alexander: you tell me who's the real conservative.

Signally, conservatives were spectacularly indifferent to the source of Alexander's wealth. Making millions off daycare—separating infants from mothers for eight hours a day, five days a week: as the abortionist says whilst laving his hands in disinfectant, "It's a living." (I had figured Alexander for an automaton when, after noticing that his Nashville office was next door to that of Glen Campbell on Music Row, I asked him what the Wichita Lineman was like and he said that he'd never bothered to meet him.)

As Debs, Chute & Jones understood, the most ennobling work we do is seldom remunerated in greenbacks. Bearing and raising a child, cultivating a garden, just being there for a sibling or friend to lean on: this "work" is compensated in a currency far more valuable than Uncle Sam's paper. This, in fact, is the work that should be honored on Labor Day. The work we do for "nothing." (For everything, really.) The work that enriches us as human beings; that binds us to our families and our neighbors; that shrouds even the most commonplace of lives in glory. This is the work whose coin, whose only coin, is love.

For as Karl Hess wrote me in November 1989, "The older I get (and I'm now, at 67, an official SENIOR although still an intellectual juvenile) the more I appreciate the work of being in love as being superior to anything else. At least that has been my experience."

Hess, one of the supplest and most creative political thinkers of the last generation, would die less than five years later on the same day, April 22, 1994, that Richard M. Nixon shuffled off to, well, you know where.

Karl's memorial service in Kearneysville, West Virginia, was attended by zero living presidents, which was apt for a man whose conscience impelled him to quit the Power he once had served.

Karl was born to a headstrong Washington, D.C., mother and a footloose Filipino millionaire. He quit school at age fifteen and worked for a dizzying succession of newspapers and magazines, including a stint as an editor of *Newsweek*. He was a sharp political operator, a free-swinging GOP polemicist, and coauthor of the 1960 platform on which Richard M. Nixon ran.

He hit it off with an Arizona senator named Barry Goldwater, whose chief speechwriter he became. "Goldwater Finds His Sorenson," declared Murray Kempton in the *New Republic*, but nary a New Frontier inanity can compete with "I would remind you that extremism in the defense of liberty is no vice. And let me remind you, also, that moderation in the pursuit of justice is no virtue."

Goldwater got swamped, and as we bogged down in the Big Muddy, Hess reassessed his Republican Party, his hireling status, his personal-parking-space life. "Vietnam," he said, "should remind all conservatives that whenever you put your faith in big government, for any reason, sooner or later you wind up as an apologist for mass murder."

Like Thoreau, Karl Hess quit. He grew a beard, donned a workshirt and combat boots, learned to use an acetylene torch, and took up welding and revolution. Reckoning that the best qualities of the Right of his boyhood—its cranky individualism, quasi-pacifist isolationism, and Main Street decentralism—had been purged, he rushed headlong—heedlessly, perhaps—into the New Left.

In his best essay, "An Open Letter to Barry Goldwater" in the New Left magazine *Ramparts*, Hess urged his old boss, whom he termed "the most essentially honest and potentially radical major American political figure," to join Students for a Democratic Society. Goldwater declined, though in his 1968 Senate campaign he had told a no doubt betwizzled crowd at the University of Arizona that he had "much in common with the anarchist wing of SDS," notably opposition to the draft and hostility to overgrown institutions.

Hess's pitch to Goldwater was a cocktail of flattery and challenge. Hadn't the senator ever wondered why "the largest corporations . . . so strenuously opposed you and supported Johnson . . . ? Could it have been that you might not have played ball quite so well as he?"

He even fit Goldwater for a dashiki. "Senator, if you had been born black, and poor, you would now be a Panther or I seriously misjudge the strength of your character and convictions."

He concluded, "I will have to admit that there is not exactly a long line queued up on the New Left waiting to hear from you. But there's a hell of a lot more room for you over here . . . than in a Republican Party which regards Everett Dirksen as a hero and you as a maverick."

Goldwater stayed put. But he also stayed friends with Karl Hess. There is an enduring image of Karl at his shaggiest protesting the war outside the Capitol; word was that the demonstration might turn violent, so even the antiwar members of Congress kept their distance. Only one politician showed up: Senator Barry Goldwater, who waded through the throng, parting the astonished crowd—a truly Red sea?—and asking the demonstrators, "Where's Karl? Where's Karl Hess?"

They met. They shook hands in the midst of the tumult—two old friends, divided by politics, but wise enough to know that politics are ephemeral, and that the real thing, the lasting thing, is friendship. Harding and Debs, Jones and Taft, Hess and Goldwater. Yes, Rodney King, we *can* all get along.

After a psychedelic stay in a floating houseboat commune on the Anacostia River, Karl and his wife, Therese, moved to West Virginia, where they lived in a home Karl built largely from scavenged materials. The visionary, the dreamer, the theorist of revolution spent the last twenty of his seventy years as a concerned neighbor, a loving husband, and the most practical of anarchists. He never lost his faith in his Dear America, either. "I continue to insist on the great and bright possibilities, the American possibilities," he wrote in 1978. "We are a varied, inventive, often idiosyncratic people. Although we may appear from time to time to worship authority . . . it still seems safe to say that most of us are antiauthoritarian by deep cultural background."

As the world went to hell, Karl Hess marched zestfully in the other direction. His obituary, by the way, ran in the nether regions of the *New York Times*, back with the lingerie ads; news of Richard M. Nixon's death dominated the front page. As for which man was the truer patriot . . . I have my suspicions.

So do the homonymic fates. Norman Rockwell's model for *Freedom of Speech*, his stirring image of American grassroots democracy, taken from an Arlington, Vermont, town meeting, was a gas station owner named . . . Carl Hess.

I don't know if a black and poor Barry Goldwater would have joined the Panthers, though he certainly would have agreed with their rejection of gun control. But a real Panther, Eldridge Cleaver, whatever his sins— and they were many, including, unforgivably, rape—put his (trigger) finger on the problem:

> There aren't any more state governments. We have these honorary pigs like Mayor Alioto or whoever your mayor might be here, presiding over the distribution of a lot of federal funds. He's plugged into one gigantic system, one octopus spanning the continent from one end to the other, reaching its tentacles all around the world, in everybody's pocket and around everybody's neck. We just have one octopus. A beast with his head wherever LBJ might be tonight. That's all we have: one monstrosity that has to be dealt with on the local level, on the state level, on the national level, on the international level.

Like the Outlaws' twenty-minute version of "Green Grass and High Tides," a lot of this goes a little way. But this was more than just Eldridge's bad-nigger bluster.

I interviewed a penitent Cleaver for *Reason* in 1985. My co-interlocutor was Lynn Scarlett, who had met the Black Panther in 1971 during his Algerian exile. Lynn, to my astonishment, later served as deputy secretary of the interior in the administration of George W. Bush. Oh well. At least it wasn't the Ministry of Interior. Cleaver's Berkeley apartment, by the way, was easy to find: 'twas the only one flying an American flag. When the greying Panther absented himself to take a leak—or a snort; he was arrested shortly thereafter—we scanned his files. He had a thick one on the possibility that Jim Morrison was still alive.

I liked Cleaver, not least for his answer to my final question:

> ME: In exile, you rued the fact that your son didn't play football. Does he play now?

> CLEAVER: He's a hell of a football player! I brainwashed him from the time he was a baby. I had a pair of football shoes that I always kept hanging in my den. These football shoes were mine at Abraham Lincoln High School in Los Angeles. I never had a chance to use them, because I got busted. But I always kept them. My son has them now, and from the time that he was first born I always talked to him about football. He loves football.

Funny thing. If baseball, the greatest of sports, is commonly regarded as the game of intellectuals—annoying eggheads wearing Red Sox and Cubs hats and throwing like girls—then football is the sport of the lunkhead, the lamebrain, the brawny illiterate. Poets and novelists—Donald Hall, Marianne Moore, Bernard Malamud—find beauty and metaphor in baseball; the football novel, by contrast, occupies less shelf space than hockey haiku. (Or the hockey novels written by Neil Young's father.)

Yet football, however unpoetic, has been the sport of American politicians, and even the odd political intellectual. Why this should be is something of a mystery, for football is committee meetings punctuated by violence, while government is . . . well, perhaps it's not so mysterious. Henry Adams once defined politics as the systematic organization of hatreds; Vince Lombardi would have understood. (The Green Bay Packers coach was a Bobby Kennedy Democrat, though his wife Marie was an America First isolationist.)

Playing college football was a virtual prerequisite for the Republican presidents of postwar, pre-millennium America: Whittier's Nixon, Ford of the Michigan Wolverines, Eureka's Reagan, and Eisenhower of West Point. To his lifelong regret, a knee injury (against Tufts, of all powderpuffs) relegated Ike, whom the *New York Times* deemed "one of the most promising backs in Eastern football," to the West Point cheerleading squad, where he huzzahed on the Black Knights of the Hudson decades before cheerleading senator Trent Lott shook his pom-poms for Ole Miss.

Before his political career even began, Gerald Ford had to choose between football and politics, and he selected the former: in 1940 Ford resigned from the original executive committee of the antiwar America First Committee because he feared that his involvement might jeopardize his position as assistant football coach at Yale. A profile in courage he was not.

Decades before former Buffalo Bills quarterback Jack Kemp spoke of football as a solvent of racial hostility, another America Firster, New York Republican congressman Hamilton Fish, a Walter Camp All-American tackle at Harvard who had commanded an infantry unit of black troops in the First World War, acted as a congressional ombudsman for black America.

Football intellectuals are rarer than gridiron politicos but commoner than drop kicks. Pro Football Hall of Fame coach Marv Levy of the Buffalo Bills is a Harvard M.A. who was beloved by his players for stumping them with pregame-speech references to such obscure historical figures as Winston Churchill. A previous Anglophile, University of Rochester president Alan Valentine, made his reputation in the 1930s as a biographer of British diplomats after earning honorable mention from Walter Camp as a lineman for that oxymoron known as the (now defunct) Swarthmore football team. Valentine, too, was an eloquent supporter of America First.

But the sport's greatest contribution to American intellectual life was Vernon Parrington, author of *Main Currents in American Thought* (1927–30), the towering three-volume history of American literature whose sweep and style have yet to be matched.

A classic American autodidact, Parrington was a Kansas farmboy and former semiprofessional baseball player in the Kansas League who hated every minute of his Harvard education, except those glorious hours he spent reading on his own in the library. Repatriated to the Dust Bowl, he taught English at the University of Oklahoma and walked the sidelines in a tweed suit and tie as the school's second football coach.

"Everything Parrington touched he seemed to vitalize," marveled one chronicler of Sooner football. Between 1897 and 1900 he compiled a record of 9-2-1, which ranks him behind only the somewhat less scholarly Sooner coaches Barry Switzer (also an author, ahem) and Bud Wilkinson.

Parrington, a William Jennings Bryan populist, was a leftist exception to the generally Republican coloration of footballers. His fellow OU coach Wilkinson was more typical: after coaching the Sooners from 1947 to 1963, winning three national championships, Wilkinson ran for the U.S. Senate in 1964 as an Oklahoma Republican. Talk about bad timing: Coach Wilkinson was hobbled by the Goldwater landslide and lost narrowly to the intermittently interesting Fred Harris, who was one-third sparkling Vernon Parrington populist and two-thirds LBJ hack.

Ah, we have drifted a ways from Maine, I suppose, but then Vernon Parrington was said by his fellow Emporian William Allen White to have thrown a mean curveball. And isn't the curveball, the naked reverse, even—

dare I say it—the old Statue of Liberty play about all we have left as the game winds down?

John Steinbeck's *The Grapes of Wrath* (1939), however passé it may be in the nation's English departments, is among the Great American Novels, and I cannot think of Ma Joad—in the flesh of Jane Darwell, for John Ford's film, though substantially more socialist-minded than Steinbeck's novel, is indelible—without thinking, too, of the Chutes in their parlous condition.

There is a memorable scene in *The Grapes of Wrath* in which a tenant farmer confronts the man evicting him from his shack:

> "It's mine. I built it. You bump it down—I'll be in the window with a rifle. You even come too close and I'll pot you like a rabbit."
>
> "It's not me. There's nothing I can do. I'll lose my job if I don't do it. And look—suppose you kill me? They'll just hang you, but long before you're hung there'll be another guy on the tractor, and he'll bump the house down. You're not killing the right guy."
>
> "That's so," the tenant said. "Who gave you orders? I'll go after him. He's the one to kill."
>
> "You're wrong. He got his orders from the bank. The bank told him, 'Clear those people out or it's your job.'"
>
> "Well, there's a president of the bank. There's a board of directors. I'll fill up the magazine of the rifle and go into the bank."
>
> The driver said, "Fellow was telling me that the bank gets orders from the East. The orders were, 'Make the land show profit or we'll close you up.'"
>
> "But where does it stop? Who can we shoot? I don't aim to starve to death before I kill the man that's starving me."

We are not starvelings, and we know whom to shoot. (Figuratively speaking, of course. We should obey the example of Dorothy Day and leave murder as an instrument of policy to the governments of the world.) The octopus must be slain, starting with its most dangerous tentacles (abolish the Department of Homeland Security, repeal the PATRIOT Act, slash the war budget and bring home our troops—from everywhere, strip absentee owners of TV and radio stations, and then in the second hour . . .) This train may not be bound for glory, but at least we're not going to Pyonyang or Baghdad or Damascus.

I like to think of Mother Jones handing the baton to Carolyn Chute as Karl Hess hums the Who. Hey you patriots of all bloodlines, you Tacoma sons of Wobblies and Nebraska daughters of Grangers and Tuskegee sons of Booker T. and Chicago daughters of America Firsters: let's get together before we get much older.

But then that's the problem, isn't it? We get older, we get no wiser, the wars of FDR and Truman turn into the wars of Kennedy and Nixon, the Gulf War of Bush I reappears as the Gulf War of Bush II, and we the people never do get together, except as atomized watchers of *Desperate Housewives*. We are, in the main, sitting fat and happy in what Robert Nisbet, in his splendid *The Quest for Community*, called "the heart of totalitarianism": for we are "the masses; the vast aggregates who are never tortured, flogged, or imprisoned, or humiliated; who instead are cajoled, flattered, stimulated by the rulers; but who are nonetheless relentlessly destroyed as human beings, ground down into mere shells of humanity." The totalitarian, wrote Nisbet, seeks "the incessant destruction of all evidences of spontaneous, autonomous association," leaving us a mass of anchorless individuals whose wasted lives are lighted only by the hideous bluish glare of the TV set.

Hey, what's on tonight?

CHAPTER SIX

Sanford 'n Seth

Or, What I Found While Hunting Civil War Artifacts in My Backyard

"We Americans are digging for art and for intellect in Troy, in Sardis and in Egypt. Let us sometimes also dig in the old records of our own towns; and, while doing so, let us pray that mind be given us to understand what we bring to light."

—John Jay Chapman

Various of the towns of Wyoming County, New York, were in the nineteenth century known as "Niggerville," which is kinda funny when you consider that the 2000 U.S. Census fixed at twenty the sum of African-Americans in Warsaw, the 3,814-strong county seat and the focus of our attention. Oh, there is a coffle of maybe 5,000 black men about ten miles north of Warsaw in Attica State Prison, but this lovely county's harsh—yet ennobling—sobriquet predates the gaol by the better part of a century. As if to emphasize its splendid contrariness, Warsaw has almost no Poles, either. The county has 43,424 persons but 49,500 cows, making it the bovine capital of New York.

Wyoming was Niggerville when Niggerville wasn't cool. It was Niggerville when that *meant* something, when "Nigger" was an acidic term of contempt meant to keep a serf class in its place and not just an exsanguinated old epithet which the prissy statues of Big Media now daintily refer to as "the n-word," as if two such filthy syllables were not fit to pass the pure lips of, say, Deborah Norville.

Warsaw, county seat of Niggerville, was the red hot center of American abolitionism, well before the notion that Africans ought not to spend their lives as bondsmen had achieved widespread currency. Of course now we're *all* abolitionists, aren't we, since virtue is so easily assumed in retrospect.

Especially in New England, which historically has embraced the Negro with all the righteous fervor of the Negroless. While New England towns fabricate tales of their Underground Railroads and white-out their slave-trading pasts, drawing liberally from that endless and endlessly annoying Yankee reservoir of moral superiority, Warsaw's nobility is hard-earned and casually worn. More than any small town in America, Warsaw deserves the title of the Cradle of American Abolitionism.

Birthplace of the abolitionist Liberty Party in 1839; home of Augustus Frank, the congressman who shepherded the antislavery Thirteenth Amendment through the House; disrespecter of the Fugitive Slave Act and a vital stop on the Underground Railroad (the real one, not the Disneyfied phantom); Warsaw was, pound for pound, the most abolitionist town in America. Her heritage is one that hundreds of far more affluent and historically compromised towns (like the homes of the Massachusetts slave-ship captains and traders) would kill for. Even from a distance of a century and a half, the Warsavian style—radical resistance to unjust authority flowing naturally in a town of front porches and ice-cream socials—beguiles. It also provides an inspiring model for a new American resistance to the expanding, minatory, and deeply un-American Empire whose subjects we have all become. Squint hard enough and you can almost read the writing on the tombstone of the Department of Homeland Security.

———

May I first tell you about Millard Fillmore? What, you say you have to leave now? Please, sit still. Just for a minute. I promise. You see, Millard matured just a dozen miles west of Warsaw, and though I won't jive you with any sonorously silly (shall we just use the adjective "McCullough-esque?") claim that the hills echo his name, I must explain why Fillmore, *pace* everyone else who has ever expressed an opinion on the subject, was a fine if not outstanding president, why his sole misstep sanctified Wyoming County, and why I can hear Rosemary Clooney belting out "Oh yes we need a little Millard!" as we lose ourselves and our country in the roseless but very thorny Bushes.

Millard Fillmore, who came of age as a scrambling young lawyer in nearby East Aurora, was an exemplary ex-president and an underrated president, and his very underrating tells us what we need to know about those noxious Schlesingerian polls of historians who Grade the Presidents. The bloodletters are great, the wagers of smaller wars are near-great, the fitful bombers are average, and the men of peace are below average or poor.

And so stands Millard in the anteroom of American history.

Fillmore, an essentially provincial man (and I use the adjective as a compliment) who had been bored to tears serving as New York's comptroller before being plucked to fame by the Whiggish fates, is given grudging credit for doing more than any president before or quite possibly since to establish trade with the Far East, and that's about it for his plus column in history's ledger.

But I will tell you a secret: Millard Fillmore ranks with the Quaker Herbert Hoover as the most pacific president in our history. Before going oval, Fillmore had opposed the disgraceful Mexican War. As president he resisted, with grit and principle, the Democrat expansionists and proto-imperialists who wished the U.S. to annex Cuba. And in retirement, he was a Peace Whig, opposed to both Lincolnian bellicosity and the tantrums of Southern fire-eaters. Millard Fillmore consistently stood for peace, for noninterference in the affairs of other nations, and for a U.S. diplomacy that was based on John Quincy Adams's dictum that "Wherever the standard of freedom and independence has been or shall be unfurled, there will be America's heart, her benedictions, and her prayers. But she does not go abroad in search of monsters to destroy. She is the well-wisher to the freedom and independence of all. She is the champion and vindicator only of her own."

President Fillmore is most reviled today for signing the Fugitive Slave Act and thus sullying the Compromise of 1850. Given that Fillmore was no craven doughface, no bootlicker of the slavocracy, but rather had been an ally of Rep. John Quincy Adams in his noble 1830s battles to permit the Congress to receive abolitionist petitions, President Fillmore's signing of the act cannot be called characteristic. Despite William Lloyd Garrison's crack that Fillmore was "as pliant a piece of dough as was ever handled," the president was simply acting out of thralldom to the sacred Union to which Abraham Lincoln would later sacrifice so many American boys. He may have been misguided—I think he was; like Garrison, I'd have said to hell with the Union—but it ill behooves our Lincolnophiliac historians to malign Millard for going the extra (whipcracking) mile to save the Union.

He also takes hits for his American (Know-Nothing) Party candidacy for president in 1856, but this was really more a case of a desperate politico jumping aboard the first passing carriage. While the Know-Nothings knew much about the ethnic groups they wished to exclude from U.S. citizenship—the Irish and others inclined to papacy—Fillmore hadn't an anti-Catholic bone in his body. In fact, Bishop Timon of Buffalo regarded him as the candidate friendliest to Catholicism in that 1856 race. Millard was no bigot; it's just that the old boy missed the political ring and would hitch a ride thereunto with any available bandwagon. He won a respectable 22 percent of the nationwide popular vote but posthumous opprobrium in his fling as a Know-Nothing.

Yeah, Fillmore foolishly took the Know-Nothing oath (which he privately regarded as "puerile"), and the episode does him no credit, but as none other than Pat Moynihan conceded in our bibulous Syracuse reunion, there really *was* an Irish problem. (In the Five Points of Manhattan, that is: Irish immigrants into the rural heartland—like, say, the Garraghans and McGuires of Western New York—were exemplary Americans from the minute they debarked from the boat.)

And let us not ignore Fillmore's dreaminess. Not as dreamboat, though Queen Victoria is said to have remarked that he was the handsomest man she had ever met. (We men of the Niagara Frontier do incline to a certain comeliness.) What I mean is that he predicted that Buffalo would be the Venice of its age, and to hasten its cultural maturation he not only founded the Buffalo Historical Society but also read Shakespeare to toiling shop hands. Fillmore was given to strange, affecting gestures, but then what do you expect from a Unitarian conciliator of the South?

(Buffalo, alas, never requited Fillmore's affection. The city fathers tore down Fillmore's mansion in 1923, though he is feted in East Aurora, which never forgot its resident president. Her tipplers gather every January 7 to toast their nativist son.)

If Fillmore's dreams of Buffalonian splendor came a cropper, he did anticipate the sanguinarily epochal event in Wyoming County's history: the September 1971 riot at Attica State Prison in which eleven guards and other employees and thirty-two inmates died after Governor Nelson Rockefeller's disastrous order to New York state police to storm the prison. Rocky probably could have ended the standoff peacefully had he bothered to speak face-to-face with the inmates—as prisoners, hostages, families, and negotiators begged him to do—but his exquisite physical cowardice kept him in Albany. Besides, the soon-to-die were a gaggle of black felons and rural working-class white guards, just the sort who would have no appreciation whatsoever of abstract expressionism.

Not to worry, though: the coven of foundations that the Rockefeller family endowed so philanthropically—and tax-avoidance-consciously—have ensured that the priapic dyslexic's brutalities are being "put into context," i.e., erased by Clio's delete key, so that generations yet unborn will know only Rocky the irrepressible, the hi-ya-fella backslapper (whose greatest public enthusiasms were for imperialism abroad and urban-renewal-in-the-service-of-modernist-architecture at home) who was Friend to All, especially the Negro, whose brethren he so sedulously committed to Corbusier-ugly housing projects. Thanks, Rocky!

A better man, Millard Fillmore, despaired of any just and peaceful solution to what liberals would later refer to so clumsily as "the race problem." In a haunting draft of his final state-of-the-union message, President Fillmore forecast civil war between blacks and whites, "a conflict of races with all the lamentable consequences which must characterize such a strife. . . . The terrific scenes of St. Domingo are sooner or later to be re-enacted here, unless something be done to avert it."

By "something" he did not mean a sectional war that would leave 600,000 men dead and the mighty rivers of America running red with blood. Rather, he urged colonization of free blacks in Africa or the West Indies. He expected slaveowners to take heed and manumit their own chattel, presenting the faithful servant not with a gold watch but a steerage-class ticket to Liberia. That many of these Negroes, citizens or no, had roots in America a century or more deep—that they were by any definition more "American" than most white Americans, including Fillmore supporters—did not trouble Millard overly much. He called for the deportation of "100,000 per annum." Their place in peonage would be taken by the Asians whose immigration he welcomed—peculiarly for a future Know-Nothing. But the important thing was to separate the black and white races, the "only sure mode of relieving the country from the increasing evil without violence and bloodshed."

Thomas Jefferson was of the same mind. As he wrote in 1821,

> Nothing is more certainly written in the book of fate than that these people are to be free. Nor is it less certain that the two races, equally free, cannot live in the same government. Nature, habit, opinion has drawn indelible lines of distinction between them. It is still in our power to direct the process of emancipation and deportation peaceably and in such slow degree as that the evil will wear off insensibly, and their place be *pari passu* filled up by free

white laborers. If on the contrary it is left to force itself on, human nature must shudder at the prospect held up.

As a sentimental liberal integrationist on matters racial, I cringe at Fillmore's doleful prophecy that "it is clear that the two races cannot long continue to subsist together," for we are sooner or later to "wade through seas of blood" in a civil war that would end in "the utter extermination of the black race." Ebony and ivory, Millard, together they learn to see the light . . . the beautiful light. Though our neighbors held hostage at Attica might beg to differ.

At this uncomfortable juncture may I blow my own horn of racial plenty? I hereby assert my claim to the record for having voted for the most African-American candidates for office in the executive branch of the U.S. government. To wit: I voted for Jesse Jackson in the Democratic primaries of 1984 and 1988, Ezola Foster (Pat Buchanan's running mate) in the 2000 general election, and Al Sharpton in the 2004 Democratic primary. I only regret that I was too young to cast a vote for Shirley "Unbought and Unbossed" Chisholm in the 1972 Democratic primaries, though if memory serves I was pulling for Dr. Spock in that year of my pre-adolescence. (Thirty-plus years hence, the left-wing Spock would be persona non grata in the Democracy, what with his skepticism of daycare and forthright opposition to war.)

Millard Fillmore conceded that "[w]ere the question now for the first time presented, whether slavery should be introduced into the Republic, there would, beyond all doubt, be an overwhelming majority against it. But it is here."

But it is here. Thus sighs Millard Fillmore, chairman of the Resignation Party.

Warsavians resigned, en masse, from *that* party.

"He named in his mind the towns he had worked through. Portage, Castile, Perry, Warsaw, Alexander. 'Warsaw,' he said to himself again, almost aloud. It was a strange name, neither pleasant nor unpleasant, exactly; interesting. Like the town itself. An old town set in the pocket of high wooded hills like mountains."

—JOHN GARDNER, The Sunlight Dialogues

We drive into the Warsaw Cemetery just south of the village looking for the graves of the noble Warsavians. Augustus Frank Jr. greets us just inside the entrance, though I am thrown for a moment when, catercorned to Frank, I spy the stone of Anson Williams. Potsie! I didn't know you were dead!

O Happy Day—this Anson Williams lived from 1802 to 1892. And despite our friend Bart Dentino breaking into a dolorous chorus of "I don't feel good," the James Brown in the cemetery's backlot is not Him either.

James Brown, Anson Williams, William Cullen Bryant: the Tinker to Evers to Chance of American culture. Bryant is our poet laureate—our Nipsey Russell, you might say—of cemeteries. His precociously morbid poem "Thanatopsis" once confounded American schoolchildren back in those prelapsarian days before mandatory "diversity" drove off the entire nineteenth century and left our daughters with the belief that the Revolutionary and Civil Wars were fought primarily by runaway slaves and girls dressed as boys.

Dear friends were with us, some who sleep
Beneath the coffin lid:
What pleasant memories we keep
Of all they said and did!

The thanatologist would be pleased that Warsaw is embracing, once more, its dead, especially the Congressmen Augustus Frank Jr. and Seth M. Gates.

Rep. Frank lived at that bloody if remunerative crossroads where Republican warmaking met Republican moneymaking. His father, a physician, had been a delegate to the founding conventions of the American Anti-Slavery Society and the New York Anti-Slavery Society. (The American Anti-Slavery Society called for "secession from the present United States government" in May 1844, consistent with the Garrisonian injunction "no union with slaveholders." Alas, when the severance came, antislavery men overcame their pacific scruples and bawled for blood and union.)

Dr. Frank Sr. was a temperance man, too, but good works were not the half of his activities: the enterprising doctor was a partner in "sawmills, grist-mills, factories, and furnaces," and "[h]e bought village lots and erected buildings on them for sale or to rent." A nineteenth-century historian of Warsaw averred, "Probably so large an amount of village property has passed through the hands of no other citizen; nor has any other rented to occupants so many stores, shops, and dwellings."

Dr. Frank was a Presbyterian, and it was within his church that the Liberty Party was conceived, if not delivered, when on November 13, 1839, he and his confreres in the Western New York Anti-Slavery Society met to nominate James G. Birney, the Kentucky abolitionist, for president.

Dr. Frank built the grandest home Warsaw has ever seen—now the law office of Charlotte Smallwood-Cook and our friend Jane Schmieder, whose father, Congressman Barber Conable, would set the standard for statesmanship in the U.S. House of Representatives. Smallwood-Cook, who in 1949 became the first elected female district attorney in New York, tells me, "Warsaw has grown intellectually because it is so isolated. People had to provide their own art and stimulation. A lot of interesting people come here to hide." The Franks hid fugitive slaves, but they were never the shy, retiring sort.

Augustus Frank Jr. multiplied the family fortune through his service as a director and vice president of the Buffalo and New York City Railroad. Elected to Congress in 1858, the younger Frank left his mark as a sponsor of, first, a graduated income tax to fund the war; and second, as floor manager of the Thirteenth Amendment to outlaw slavery. Missions accomplished, he came home in 1865 and spent the next three decades battening on a series of railroad and bank directorships. He had done good, and he had done well. The postwar railroads directed by this abolitionist were quite above-ground.

War is the health of the state, as the percipient hunchback Randolph Bourne famously aphorized, and if the neo-Confederate critics of Lincoln's War willfully ignore the racist "I'm not gonna fight for niggers" aspect of the antiwar Democrat cause, the eulogists of Father Abraham, for whom Frank delivered a stemwinding speech in Washington City in May 1860, gloss over the extent to which the Civil War enshrined industrial capitalism, the subordination of the states to the federal behemoth, and such odiously statist innovations as conscription, the jailing of war critics, and the income tax of Augustus Frank Jr.

Seth M. Gates lies within hectoring distance of the Franks in the Warsaw Cemetery. Gates, an attorney, organized an August 1835 abolitionist meeting in Le Roy which ended with a stoning, a drenching, the smashing of windows, and the hurling of a twelve-foot hemlock plank into a church basement. Undaunted, Gates convened 100 delegates at a March 1836 meeting in Batavia whose purpose was "convincing all our citizens . . . that Slavery was a crime in the sight of God, a perpetual violation of his law, and the best interests of all concerned required its immediate abandonment."

A mob broke up this conclave with "the blowing of horns and whistles, the jingling of bells and unearthly howlings." Gates, who had begun his political career as an Anti-Mason, was relatively unfazed by such mummery. Nor did horns and whistles disturb his peace, for Gates, too, was a railroad bug, a promoter of the failed Warsaw and Le Roy Railroad.

Two years after the Batavia mob shouted him down, Seth Gates was elected to Congress as a Whig. He achieved a certain notoriety by mailing abolitionist pamphlets under his frank, a practice that led Savannah, Georgia, planter A. Wilkins to put a price of $500 on his head.

William Lloyd Garrison praised Gates as

> uncompromising for the right, faithful to a sensitive and an enlightened conscience, devoid of all fear of the Adversary and his machinations, strong in the conflict of freedom with oppression, serene and confident in the midst of fiery trial and deadly perils, untainted by selfish consideration, choosing to be popularly misunderstood and maligned rather than to be false to his conviction of duty to God, his fellowmen and his country, patriotic in the purest sense of the term and noble in his aims and ambitions.

He was Jesus Christ with a trunk full of railroad stocks.

Gates, as was the custom then if not, regrettably, today, came home from Congress in 1843, finally earning his political reward when President Lincoln gave him the postmastership of Warsaw in 1861. He died in 1877, having done, as the minister said at his funeral, "his duty to God, who had made of one blood all nations of man, and the teachings of the Master who directed his followers to do as they would be done by, bade him to strike as best he could against the fetters on the limbs of his brothers."

His sisters, too. One of them—Eliza by name, and in fact a Stoweaway—is buried next to her husband William Burghardt several paces west of Seth Gates. Burghardt, an African-American barber in the Warsaw of the 1850s, is—or so we like to believe—kin to W. E. B. DuBois, whose B stands for Burghardt. Eliza, his wife, was smuggled northward to freedom in 1850. Eliza's hegira with her mother, Mary, via wagon, and their subsequent protection by the townspeople of Warsaw in defiance of the Fugitive Slave Act, is a vitalizing legend dramatized for its bicentennial by Warsavian Harvey Granite in his play *The Woman in the Box*. This is no fantasy spun by guilt-ridden Bay Staters whose Vineyard cottages were paid for with blood money. Wyoming County had genuine heroes; her thirteen Underground Railroad stationmasters were second in New York only to the far larger county of Monroe, home of Frederick Douglass.

The handsome stone marking the resting place of Eliza and William Burghardt was the doing, in part, of Jane Schmieder, whose Conable ancestors anchor the northeast corner of the Warsaw Cemetery. Jane and her husband Bernie are the parents of five adoptive children, all African-American or mixed race, and let me tell you those Schmieder kids were a godsend when it came time to cast *The Woman in the Box*.

I wrote at length about Barber B. Conable Jr., Jane's father, in *Dispatches from the Muckdog Gazette* (2003), which all reasonably literate Americans have read. Thus I will say only that Conable, born to poetry-reciting judges and dairy farmers in sylvan Wyoming County and twenty years (1965–85) the Republican congressman from our district, was the finest statesman Upstate New York has ever produced.

Pat Moynihan esteemed him beyond any other member of Congress. Indeed, during one fall campaign, the Genesee County Republicans and Democrats held rallies in adjacent hotels. Moynihan was at the Democratic gathering, and after he spoke he wandered over to the Republican rally. The senator ambled up to the platform, took the microphone, said simply, "Congress without Barber Conable is *unthinkable!*" and left. That he was probably three or even six sheets to the wind does not mean that he did not mean it.

I remember the penultimate time I spoke with my friend Barber Conable. We had just taped a two-hour chat in which he mused, autobiographically, earnestly, self-effacingly, plaintively, about his extraordinary career.

"You wanna get me before I'm dead?" Conable asked. "No, no, nothing that morbid," I lied. After the videotaping we sat outside, overlooking his backyard forest, a bosky wonderland of more than 170 varieties of trees he had planted, many of them exotic species obtained during his presidency of the World Bank. I gave him names of politicos of my era (and his) and he offered frank assessments. For instance, of a fellow New York Republican: "the kind of jackass who arrives at the State of the Union three hours early so he can get an aisle seat and be seen shaking hands with the president." Do we really need to know anything more about such a fool?

Conable's legislative achievements, he said, were "written on sand." Revenue sharing, accelerated depreciation—you may stop yawning now— all those little tweakings of the tax code—that tax code dreamt up so long ago by Augustus Frank Jr. as a means of paying for war—have been supplanted by other tweakings.

What remains is far sturdier and more perdurable than the insubstantialities of law. It is the example set by Conable: a man of his place, deeply ethical, with a brilliant mind, biting wit, and capacious understanding.

He died November 30, 2003. His daughter Emily told me that they had read to him from my book in his final two days. I should append to this fact something self-deprecating, falsely modest, but I won't. I was moved.

There were no platitudes, no pomp, no politics at Barber Conable's funeral. About seventy-five of us, precious few powerbrokers but plenty of cousins, gathered for a twenty-minute Unitarian service in a lightly falling early December snow as Barber Conable was laid to rest in the Alexander Village Cemetery, surrounded by the Schmieder's cow pasture. Lucine and I tossed a shovelful of dirt on the casket. Our county's greatest man, gone.

Barber Conable was not a Unitarian, just a non-believer who appreciated the culture and forms of rural churches. He was in good company: Millard Fillmore was a Unitarian. Conable owned furniture from the Millard Fillmore collection, no mean acquisition given that poor Millard is usually remembered as the man who introduced the bathtub into the White House. (He didn't really. It was a Menckenian hoax.) William

Howard Taft was the last Unitarian president; his son, Robert, Mr. Republican but not Mr. Trinitarian, played golf Sunday mornings.

The Unitarian minister at the Conable service quoted the great nineteenth-century atheist Robert Ingersoll, a selection perhaps justified by recalling that Ingersoll, who dubbed James Blaine "the plumed knight" and once advertised a cigar with the skeptical slogan "Let us smoke in this world—not in the next," was an Upstater by birth and *the* silver-tongued Republican orator of the Gilded Age. It is inconceivable today that the GOP's most popular speaker would be the nation's leading atheist, a man who could write of his boyhood, "I have a dim recollection of hating Jehovah when I was exceedingly small," but there you are. Bob Ingersoll was at the cemetery that December day, but the Bushes were not. And that seemed about right.

Compare the republican simplicity of Conable's funeral with the debacle that was the 2001 burial of another Republican congressman, South Carolina's Floyd Spence, chairman of the House Armed Services Committee and a reliable shoveler of tax dollars into the Pentagon's maw. Vice President Cheney left his bunker for the nonce to attend Spence's funeral service. He was not your typical deferential mourner. Cheney demanded that Spence's dying requests—that the band play "Dixie" at his service and that a Confederate flag be displayed—be ignored. To its eternal discredit, the Spence family acceded. So they had their celebrity guest: who cares that the deceased was dishonored in death?

As the descendant of abolitionists and suffragettes, Barber Conable was unlikely to have requested "Dixie" at his obsequies. But he sure as hell didn't want the occasion marred by obsequious pols, either.

We are not in the habit of renaming our places, and wisely so, but if ever the appellation "Warsaw" wears out, I can think of no more apposite cognomen for his little village than Conable, New York.

Gerrit Smith has come down to us through history as the hypochondria-cal Upstate sugar daddy who bought John Brown his guns in 1859 and then avoided prosecution for treason with a well-timed stint in the nuthouse. Smith's posthumous reputation has, of late, taken on a glow: long disparaged as a fanatic with more money than sense, in recent years he has benefitted from the near-canonization of the abolitionists.

A Central New York land speculator whose zeal for human better-ment led him to embrace every cause from dress reform to dietary fads, Smith makes easy prey for caricaturists. But he was also a generous man with a genuine sense of civic responsibility.

Smith was so esteemed by his neighbors that he was elected to Con-gress in 1852 as an independent. He served but one truncated term, quit-ting partway through for no apparent reason other than that he felt like it. Yet in his brief career Rep. Gerrit Smith compiled a libertarian voting record that might be the envy of such legendary constitutionalist skin-flints as the late H. R. Gross (R-IA) and the great Ron Paul (R-TX).

The voters knew what they were getting in Smith. A year before the election, he published *The True Office of Civil Government*, a pamphlet in which he denied that government had any role whatever in education, transportation, mail-carrying, moral regulation, and trade.

Investing in the future? Creating an infrastructure for growth? Nur-turing children, our most valuable resource? The muzak of the modern progressive would not move Smith, who informed voters that "the build-ing of railroads and canals and the care of schools and churches fall en-tirely outside" the limits of government.

Congressman Smith walked the walk. He proposed to abolish cus-toms houses ("I am an absolute free-trade man"), West Point, and the Post Office. He voted against any and all subsidies to private enterprise and even opposed the federal distribution of seeds, for government's "sole le-gitimate office is to protect the persons and property of its subjects."

He argued for the immediate abolition of slavery on religious grounds: "Slavery is the baldest and biggest lie on earth. In reducing man to a chattel, it denies that man is man; and, in denying, that man is man, it denies, that God is God—for, in His own image, He made man—the black man and the red man, as well as the white man." Yet unlike most abolitionists, Smith was a Jeffersonian democrat who favored an agrarian society governed by a night-watchman state. Southern congressmen found him cordial—a sincere Yorker, not a sanctimonious Yankee.

Smith made a single exception to his radical libertarian voting record: he could not countenance the sale of demon rum. He voted and speechified for the banning of the traffic in spirits, all the while insisting, incongruously, that "[g]overnment is not the custodian of the people's morals." (After the war, Smith convinced prohibitionists to organize within the infelicitously named Anti-Dramshop Party. The moniker never caught on, though the cause did.)

Congressman Smith was also a virtual pacifist, decrying "the dark, barbarous, baleful spirit of war." No cause, he believed, was worth carnage: "God forbid that American slavery should come to a violent end. I hold . . . that no revolution is worth the shedding of blood." A decade later the war came, and everything changed. Like many abolitionists, he first took a "good riddance" approach to the seceding states of the Deep South, but once blood was spilled he gravely cheered on the crimson tide.

Soon Gerrit Smith was calling for conscription and the suppression of Democratic newspapers. He sneered that Lincoln "would have made a good President had he only not been trained to worship the Constitution," which Smith dismissed as "a petty thing."

"Save the Constitution in time of Peace," declared Smith. "But in time of War save the Country with or without the Constitution." The Congressman Smith of 1853 would have been appalled.

Today we remember Gerrit Smith as an apostle of war and bloodshed. The Gerrit Smith who once tried to give voice to a gentle rural American anarchism is, well, gone with the wind.

Yet I remain an ardent, yea fulsome and excessive, admirer of the early abolitionists, Smith among them, their eyes lit by the divine spark, the worst of them temperance fanatics and chronic do-gooders but the best men and women of vim and anarchy, heedless of social consequences, indifferent to political ostracism. Hell, I even like crazy old John Brown. Not the throat-slitter of Ossawatamie; no, my Brown is the brotherhood-of-man dreamer who established a hamlet for freemen in North Elba in the Adirondacks.

Unexceptional, you say. What a profile in courage I cut! Taking my stand with the abolitionists seven score years after the trampling of the grapes of wrath. What's next, Bill? A denunciation of Jim Crow? A ringing endorsement of female suffrage?

Ah, but there is a flip side. For I also honor the antiwar Democrats of the North, the execrated Copperheads who have long since been consigned to the snakepit of American history. If I would have voted Lincoln in 1860, won over by his courageous opposition to the Mexican War, I'd have cast my ballot for George McClellan in 1864. You see, I agree with the Peace Democrats that the war was a tragic mistake. No cause is worth 600,000 deaths. And the Copperheads' envenomed critique of Lincoln's assumption of dictatorial wartime powers—Old Abe made John Ashcroft and Alberto Gonzales look like Nat Hentoff—takes on a prescient luster in our age of discarded liberties and the War on Terror.

Which brings us to Dick Crozier, like Gerrit Smith a Central New Yorker, though in an incarnation that would send Mad Old John Brown in search of a machete.

As we walk down the rutted dirt road leading into the historic Batavia Cemetery on its annual Civil War candlelight tour, we halt before a somber man seated at a desk. He wears no uniform; he carries no gun. He is Ohio Congressman Clement L. Vallandigham, who claims to sit in a "military bastille for no other offense than my political opinions."

Dick Crozier is Vallandigham; the New York Republican has impersonated the Democratic dissenter since the mid-1990s. Crozier has also appeared as the congressman's bete noire, but then "anyone who's tall and has a beard gets asked to play Lincoln."

If most visitors to reenactments have never heard of Clement L. Vallandigham, Dick Crozier gives them something to think about. "I say that someday, decisions will be made not by local people but by politicians in distant Washington. People look at me and say, 'Oh, that's where it happened—that's how we ended up with this omnipotent government.'"

Clement L. Vallandigham was the lawyerly son of a Presbyterian minister. A conventional Democrat of states'-rights sympathies and a devotee of Edmund Burke, he was a friend neither to slavery ("a moral, social & political evil") nor to the Negro. Like Lincoln, Vallandigham reverenced "the Union," though he wished to preserve it by conciliation—Republicans said "appeasement"—rather than warfare.

In February 1861, one month before Abraham Lincoln took office, Rep. Vallandigham proposed amending the Constitution so as to divide the country into four sections: North, West, Pacific, and South. Presidents could be elected and controversial legislation enacted only by gaining a majority of votes from all sections.

Vallandigham's plan, with its Calhounian echoes, died aborning; war came. But whereas the leader of the Midwestern Democrats, Stephen Douglas, fell in behind Lincoln, Clement L. Vallandigham became the most outspoken antiwar voice in Congress.

The whiskers had barely curled on the president's new beard before Vallandigham was charging him with having launched "a terrible and bloody revolution" whose features were death, taxes, a swollen executive branch, and the erosion of personal liberties.

Threats and imprecations rained down on Vallandigham's head. Branded a traitor, a rival in odium to Benedict Arnold and Aaron Burr, he stood his ground. As his biographer Frank Klement writes, the congressman "was not one to be intimidated or bow to pressure. The insults hurled his way . . . only made him more defiant."

After losing his reelection bid in a gerrymandered district, Vallandigham returned to Dayton. His timing was atrocious. General Ambrose Burnside had just been demoted from commander of the Army of the Potomac to commander of the Department of the Ohio. Smarting from the humiliation, Burnside declared that war critics in his jurisdiction would be arrested and tried in military courts.

On May 1, 1863, Vallandigham publicly denounced the "wicked and cruel" war by which "King Lincoln" was "crushing out liberty and erecting a despotism." As if to prove the speaker's point, General Burnside ordered the orator arrested on charges of disloyalty.

A hastily assembled military tribunal found Vallandigham guilty. President Lincoln ordered him exiled to the Confederacy, despite Vallandigham's protest that he was a loyal "citizen of Ohio & of the United States . . . banished from my country for no other offense than love of constitutional liberty." As a staunch Union man, Vallandigham was unwelcome in the secessionist South, so Confederate blockade-runners smuggled him into Canada.

The Ohio Democratic Party gave the martyred "Valiant Val" its 1863 nomination for governor, despite his Canadian residency. The exile's electoral fate was sealed by Union victories at Gettysburg and Vicksburg, which deflated the peace movement.

Lonely for Ohio and the shouts of the crowd, Vallandigham returned to Dayton amidst great fanfare in the summer of 1864, almost daring the military authorities to arrest him. They ignored him, trusting that historians would succeed where Burnside had not.

History came through. Vallandigham rates barely a footnote today; he is remembered, if at all, as the inspiration for Edward Everett Hale's short story "The Man without a Country."

Vallandigham died in 1871 in a bizarre legal mishap. Defending an accused murderer, he was demonstrating to a room of lawyers how the deceased had accidentally shot himself. The demonstration went too well. Vallandigham picked up a pistol he believed to be bullet-less, pulled the trigger, exclaimed, "My God, I've shot myself!" and that was the end of Valiant Val.

We had our own Vallandigham, or at least our own Democratic skeptic, just up Route 98: Lieutenant Governor Sanford Church, dark-horse candidate for the Democratic presidential nomination in 1868.

Church, a Democrat in Whiggish Orleans County, served as district attorney and assemblyman before his election to the lieutenant governorship in 1850. Although linked to the noble governor Horatio Seymour, later to be lightning rod of the anti-Lincoln Democrats, Church was hardly an appeaser of the South: he had attended the 1848 Free Soil national convention in Buffalo. After the war, he was elected chief justice of the state court of appeals.

I have on our coffee table a Sanford Church speech of October 13, 1863, delivered in Batavia and titled "The Revolutionary Designs of the Abolitionists."

The "glorious Union," Church told the assemblage of Batavia Democrats, teetered on "the verge of destruction." After some hokum about laying "aside all our partisan feeling and prejudice"—always a disingenuous prolegomenon to a partisan appeal of the most tendentious sort—our man Sanny gets down to business.

The Union as it Was; The Constitution as it Is. Or so went the Democratic slogan of 1862– 63.

Church gives away the game almost before it begins, calling "the attempt forcibly to break down the authority of the Constitution over the whole country for fancied or real grievances . . . an unlawful and criminal act which cannot be justified or tolerated."

His quarrel, it seems, is not with the war, or with Lincoln's policy of Union at bayonet-point. Rather, he espies "the cloven foot of abolitionism" within the Republican tent. A war—the sacrifice of more than half a million American men and boys, the fortification of centralized government to a degree undreamt of by the founders—is fine if fought for the abstraction of Union, but if to this abstraction should be appended a flesh-and-blood goal—the emancipation of black bondsmen—then Church and the Democrats hurl anathemas all the livelong day.

Abolitionists propagate "fanatical heresies" and urge "monstrous strides towards usurpation and despotism." (Yes, they were fanatics, but I do want somewhere to give the Radical Republicans credit for wit. "It is not my appearance but my disappearance that troubles me," said Thaddeus Stevens on his deathbed. He might have said instead, "It is not the Constitution but my constitution that troubles me.")

In acquiescing to the war, "responsible" Northern Democrats like Church undermined themselves. Church vilified the Lincoln administration for seeking to "absorb, centralize and consolidate the rights and powers of the loyal States in the general government," but the United States, in their plural form, were not capable of waging an offensive war whilst observing constitutional niceties. The health of the state and all that. A weakling state is a peaceful state. It cannot fight a war of aggression without becoming a state of an altogether different order. Church can denounce "a large standing army and a ruinous system of taxation" all he wishes, and earn my huzzahs, but in denying the right of secession, of smaller bodies to break away from the larger, he has set the tyrant's plate.

The antiwar position of 1861–65 was honorable and deep-set in the old American grain. The Democrat position, anti-Lincoln but not antiwar, was incoherent, a dodge, even cowardly. So while Sanford Church scored numerous points off Lincoln in his Batavia address—predicting that someday schools will "become absorbed in the general government," defending habeas corpus—by failing to strike at the root he let grow the weed. The tools he selected were simply inadequate for the task.

The Church manse in Albion has long since been converted to a handsome funeral home—fittingly, as the states'-rights tendency within the Democracy has died and rotted, though its corpse was not even afforded the rouged cheeks and embalming fluid that are the undertaker's tools of trade.

Yet Sanford Church, father and son, still practice law on Albion's Main Street of handsome brick buildings and empty storefronts. I met "Sandy" Church, latest in the line of Sanfords and Sons (which was interrupted only by the first Sanford's son George), over breakfast at the Village House restaurant. He has graying reddish hair and a car filled with basketballs for his boy and his pals. Sandy is the first Republican Church: his dad was county Democratic chairman and once hosted Senator Moynihan on a tour of the magnificent dome-and-cupola, Greek-revival Orleans County courthouse, a very Moynihan thing to do. The senator loved stately houses of state.

Sandy, a former member of the Albion school board, is another revenant; he came home to practice after Duke Law School because he didn't want to be "on the treadmill."

So the Copperhead family stayed loyal to Albion, while the Franks and Gateses are long gone from Warsaw. Draw a lesson if you wish.

The guardians of political orthodoxy, who are more Cerberean than cerebral, are loth to permit the airing of any but the Ken Burns social studies textbook version of the Civil War. Dissent is suffocated. Radical critics, Vallandigham foremost among them, have fallen through the memory hole. Their heirs are likewise burked, even though their participation would enrich the American political debate immeasurably.

For instance, the most prominent neo-Confederate intellectuals—I think of, among others, Professor Clyde Wilson of the University of South Carolina, editor of the Calhoun papers; and Donald Livingston, Emory University professor of philosophy—in their emphasis on local rule, opposition to U.S. imperialism, and attacks on chain stores and globalism, are far closer to Gore Vidal and William Appleman Williams than to Strom Thurmond and Lester Maddox.

But they play the unheard music in a New South that is ashamed of its heritage, a New South whose vapidity is captured by that obscene motto of Atlanta: "the City Too Busy to Hate." Even more fatuous was the claim I encountered in a "Welcome to Chattanooga!" visitor's guide: "Progress and Chattanooga are synonymous." To which the dispirited traveler can only reply, "Oh, I am so sorry."

When I visited Columbia, South Carolina, in April 2005 to interview the libertarianish Republican governor Mark Sanford, I was appalled to find the circa-1890 state capitol dwarfed by the hideous SouthTrust bank skyscraper across Gervais Street. Capital over capitol, eh? The Confederate flag has been taken off the dome ("I'm for the Confederate flag flying anywhere anybody wants to fly it at any time. . . . The flag to me represents many noble things," Shelby Foote once told me, and I agree); the hidden gem that is the South Carolina Confederate Relic Room, which the state took over from the United Daughters of the Confederacy, is purposely tucked away in obscurity behind a generic dinosaurs-and-wind-experiments state museum for unimaginative children; and to rub soy sauce in the wound, I walked three hours without finding a barbecue or ribs joint. For God's sake, I ate Chinese food in the land of cavaliers and Calhoun! (Not that the capital of the Palmetto State has entirely repudiated its past: I stayed at the Mary Chesnut Bed & Breakfast, briefly the residence of the South's great diarist, who was given more to mordancy than moonlight and magnolias. Although as a solo traveler I was assigned the bridal suite, Mary's succubus kept her distance.)

I know a Confederate exiled in Illinois who threatened to redact his license plate to read "Land of Douglas." Edgar Lee Masters would have approved. The Spoon River poet and Lincoln-hater marveled that "with Douglas almost lost to the interest of biographers, he yet remains a book put aside on the shelf which some day history will take down in wonder that it should so long have been left unread."

It remains untouched on that dusty top shelf. Deservedly so, perhaps: why rehabilitate a railroad lawyer, a shifty politico, the diminutive runner-up in the dubious Mary Todd sweepstakes? The Stephen Douglas revival ought to arrive somewhere between the resurrections of Lewis Cass and Michael Dukakis.

The most spectacular crucifixion of a Civil War heretic in recent years was that of Ron Maxwell, writer-director of *Gods and Generals* (2003), the sequel by way of prequel to his well-received battle film *Gettysburg* (1993). *Gods and Generals* is so free of cant, of false notes, of the politically conformist genuflections that we expect in our historical movies, that one watches it as if in a trance, wondering if he hasn't stumbled into an alternative America wherein independents like Maxwell get $80 million from Ted Turner to make complex and beautiful films about what Gore Vidal has called "the great single tragic event that continues to give resonance to our Republic."

Gods and Generals received a handful of rhapsodic reviews (including mine in the *American Enterprise*) but far more abusive attacks, many of them politically motivated, for Maxwell's refusal to depict the Confederates in the demonic mold required by p.c. etiquette. Maxwell is that two-headed calf—an intellectual in the cinema—and his historically respectable view of the war as a struggle between an agrarian South and an industrial-capitalist North (rather than evil racists vs. purehearted saints) earned him a vilification the likes of which has not been seen since Michael Cimino (an equally nonconformist epic filmmaker) and his unfairly damned *Heaven's Gate*.

I had met Maxwell after *Gettysburg* but before *Gods and Generals*, when he read the antiwar poetry of Robinson Jeffers to a conference of the paleoconservative John Randolph Club. He was intense and articulate. But he makes *movies*, my inner haughtiness sneered. (I ought not to listen to the supercilious twit within. How I cringe to recall the phone call from a Hollywood producer when my first book, a novel, came out. He tried to chat me up and I treated him as if I were Henry James and he'd asked me to write advertising copy for Rough on Bile pills.)

Anyway, whene'er Maxwell recited Allen Tate or declaimed Shakespearean lines in conversation I reminded myself of his pre-*Gettysburg* filmography: *Little Darlings* (1980), in which Tatum O'Neal and Kristy McNichol played boy-crazy teens who had rather better luck at picking men than the actresses would in real life; and *The Night the Lights Went*

Out in Georgia (1981), an amiable country and western music–soaked character study of a feckless brother and ambitious sister that has nothing at all to do with the Vicki Lawrence novelty song from which it takes its name.

Still . . . *Little Darlings*? I bethought myself of the gap between ambition and talent: I imagined Jim "Ernest" Varney admiring *Rashomon*, or Donny Most directing a "Happy Days" episode as homage to Resnais's *Last Year at Marienbad*.

Until, that is, I saw *Gods and Generals*, which is framed, befitting its large and largely fulfilled ambitions, by an epigraph from George Eliot ("A human life, I think, should be well rooted in some spot of a native land, where it may get the love of tender kinship. . . . The best introduction to astronomy is to think of the nightly heavens as a little lot of stars belonging to one's own homestead") and, over the closing credits, Bob Dylan's haunting "Cross the Green Mountain," the death-dream of Stonewall Jackson, Dylan's plaint sounding like Appalachia by way of Hibbing, Minnesota, as abolitionist folkie meets Jewish Confederate in the great song that is America.

One of the film's signal virtues is its respect for place. In a lovely scene, Robert E. Lee (Robert Duvall) surveys the land around Fredericksburg from atop a hill before the battle. Lee explains to his adjutant that this is where he met the woman who would become his wife. He muses,

> It's something these Yankees do not understand, will never understand. Rivers, hills, valleys, fields, even towns: to those people they're just markings on a map from the war office in Washington. To us, they're birthplaces and burial grounds, they're battlefields where our ancestors fought. They're places where we learned to walk, to talk, to pray. They're places where we made friendships and fell in love. . . . They're the incarnation of all our memories and all that we love.

The critics were unmoved. Maxwell had failed to include the obligatory scene in which Robert E. Lee rapes Iman or Stonewall Jackson lynches Will Smith. Gods, generals, and Ron Maxwell were buried under an avalanche of obloquy.

The war, it seems, had claimed another victim. In Ross Lockridge's Whitmanesque novel *Raintree County* (1948), Professor Jerusalem Webster Stiles confidently predicts, "The new generations will look back on the Civil War with great calm. It's hard to feel sorry for folks who died a hundred years ago."

Sorry, professor. And sorry, Ron. You might have had better luck in advancing the froward view of Rhett Butler, who whatever his moral failings had a talent for cutting through the cant. Butler told a roomful of Margaret Mitchell's Georgians, "no matter what rallying cries the orators give to the idiots who fight, no matter what noble purposes they assign to wars, there is never but one reason for a war. And that is money. All wars are in reality money squabbles. But so few people ever realize it. Their ears are too full of bugles and drums and fine words from stay-at-home orators."

We now return to your regularly scheduled Middle Eastern war.

Ah, to hell with the gloom. Soon it will be glorious October, loveliest month of an Upstate year. Batavia, Warsaw, Elba, Albion are awash in football, cider, leaves of russet and crimson, and the pumpkin: "O,—fruit beloved of boyhood!" sang Whittier, poet of autumn and abolition.

Let the leaves dream of photosynthesis; I dream of mere synthesis—of melding, of a Warsaw autumn:

> —the rightness, the righteousness, of the Franks and Gateses, fanatics in liberty;
> —the constitutional scruples of the Copperheads, for going to Church is never wasted;
> —and the good-natured conciliatory peacemaking of Millard Fillmore, who knew that war was rapine and death, tyranny and vastation.

The fellow who could draw life from each of these three traditions might really be onto something.

Come fall I will parry Lucine's hint to rake with Stephen Vincent Benet's poetical defense of indolence in the face of leafswarms:

> *Gather the leaves with rakes,*
> *The burning autumn, Springfield,*
> *Gather them in with rakes*
> *Lest one of them turn to gold*

I use this stanza annually, disguising my laziness as poetic principledness. It buys me time till my friend, the wind, sweeps the leaves down the street, into the yards of neighbors more rakish than I.

I have altered my view of this poem since my visit to Springfield under a louring, pouring sky in late November 2004. Whilst walking Honest Abe's restored neighborhood I slipped on wet—unraked!—leaves in front of Abraham Lincoln's home and went flying ass over teakettle, muddying my pants, my shirt, my brand-new jacket.

Vachel Lindsay had Abraham Lincoln's ghost walking Springfield at midnight but I can't even stroll down its boulevard at midday without landing on my can.

I can walk through Warsaw, though. The view is spectacular. When autumn comes to the valley I sit in its cemetery. I can see far back and way ahead. Why don't you look, too? The future, unlike the dates on these graves, is never incised in stone.

Conclusion

Why I Am Not Ashamed to Be an American

"I should hate to spend the only life I was going to have here in being annoyed with the time I happened to live in."
— ROBERT FROST

I n the wake of Vietnam and Watergate, John Fogerty of the terrific (if weather-mad) band Creedence Clearwater Revival recalled "feeling this shame just sweep over me. . . . I was terribly ashamed of our country."

He needn't have been, as he soon realized. For Richard Nixon was "not my country. He's those guys—over in Washington. First thing I thought [about] was the Grand Canyon and my friends and neighbors—and the people all across the country. The people in power aren't my country any more than a bunch of gangsters are my country."

Nor is the Fortunate Son (whatever his last name happens to be) in his fortified bunker on Pennsylvania Avenue my country—or your country, either, unless you are as thin and insubstantial as one of those vapid wraiths hissing of empire on CNN or MSNBC or any of the other alphabetical collisions in our corporate-media soup.

There are two Americas: the televised America, known and hated by the world, and the rest of us. The former is a factitious creation whose strange gods include HBO, accentless TV anchorpeople, Dick Cheney, reruns of *Friends*, and the National Endowment for Democracy. It is real enough—cross it and you'll learn more than you want to know about weapons of mass destruction—but it has no heart, no soul, no connection to the thousand and one real Americas that produced Zora Neale Hurston and Jack Kerouac and Saint Dorothy Day and the Mighty Casey who has struck out.

I am of the other America, the unseen America, the America un-dreamt of by the foreigners who hate my country without knowing a single thing about it. Ours is a land of volunteer fire departments, of baseball played without payment or sanction, of uncut maples and unpasteurized cider.

So no, I do not feel "ashamed" of my country, for America, as John Fogerty understood, is not George W. Bush or Hillary Clinton but my friends, my neighbors, and yes, the Grand Canyon, too. Even better, it is the little canyon and the rude stream and Tom Sawyer's cave and all those places whose names we know, whose myths we have memorized, and whose existence remains quite beyond the compass of ABC-TV.

Yet we are the America that suffers in wartime: we do the dying, the paying of taxes, we supply the million unfortunate sons (and now daugh-ters) who are sent hither and yon in what amounts to a vast government uprooting of the populace. Militarism and empire are the enemies of small-town America, not only because some native sons come home in bodybags but also for the desolating fact that many never come home at all. They are scattered to the winds, sent out—by force or enticement of state—in the great American diaspora, never to return to the places that gave them nur-ture.

War kills the provinces, as Wendell Berry knows and tells so well. It drains them of cultural life as surely as it takes the lives of eighteen-year-old boys. I have written previously of how almost every healthy, vig-orous cultural current of the 1930s was terminated by U.S. entry into the Second World War. Vietnam, like any drawn-out war or occupation, dis-rupted normal courtship patterns on the homefront: the difference between republic and empire might be restated as the difference between taking the girl next door to the Sadie Hawkins Dance and paying a Saigon whore in chocolate bars and the Yankee dollar.

The War on Terror, which we have been assured will haunt our life-times and those of our children, has intensified my reactionary radicalism, my anarchism—my *patriotism*—and may yet redefine American politics along a natural divide: the personal versus the abstract. It may also intro-duce for the first time since the 1930s a serious strain of quasi-pacifism into our political life: not the caricatured pacifism of the Don Knotts–Phil Donahue hybrid who would stand by, paralyzed by a poisonous combina-tion of fear and self-loathing, as Kitty Genovese screams in rape-horror. Rather, this is the pacifism of Day, of place, of love of the particular.

"His sympathies were for race—too lofty to descend to persons," a wit once said of the righteously abolitionist senator Charles Sumner. For how else could a man not merely countenance but positively rejoice in the slaughter of his countrymen, not only rebel southerners but noble Robert Gould Shaw and Berkshires boys, too?

The most dangerous people—the ones who will kill you for your own good—are those who subordinate the individual to abstractions: the class, the master race, the efficient economy. They gain power because they are willing to perform the sleazy and degrading acts necessary to its achieve-ment.

Influential men, men of state, their days a blur of movement, retain-ers at beck and call, come to see others as toadies or supplicants (with the toothsome few laid aside as bed partners). In their eyes we are all expend-able. Why was anyone surprised when Ted Kennedy swam away, leaving Mary Jo Kopechne to scream in her air pocket till the water rushed in? Kopechnes serve, and Kennedys are served; Vietnam was just Chappa-quiddick with rice paddies. Shut up and die.

Who are these creatures, capable of decreeing—with no more com-punction than an acned scamp in a Metallica t-shirt displays whilst zap-ping foes in Mortal Kombat—the mass execution of, say, Iraqi children or Vietnamese peasants? Dorothy Day wrote of Hiroshima and Nagasaki:

Mr. Truman was jubilant. . . . True man. What a strange name, come to think of it. . . . Truman is a true man of his time in that he was jubilant. He was not a son of God, brother of Christ, brother of the Japanese, jubilating as he did . . . *jubilate deo.* We have killed 318,000 Japanese . . . they are vaporized, our Japanese brothers, scattered, men, women, and babies, to the four winds, over the seven seas. Perhaps we will breathe their dust into our nostrils, feel them in the fog of New York on our faces, feel them in the rain on the hills of Easton.

But then Dorothy was what they called a sob sister. Of course she wasn't: her acts of charity, her very life, were face to face, local, and intensely "personalist," as she sometimes described her philosophy. She saw Christ in the face of a Bowery bum, and like an impractical idealist she offered him bread instead of a knee to the groin and an application for food stamps.

The *New York Tribune* observed of General Ulysses S. Grant's "immobile, heavy, and expressionless" visage that it was "the face of the only man in America, perhaps, who could make the calculation of the multitude of lives necessary to blot out a multitude of other lives." This calculus requires a certain moral density; an inability to credit persons unknown to you with lives, families, feelings, and histories of their own. Politicians, who perforce see people merely as an agglomeration of lever-pullers and chad-punchers called the "electorate," are capable of making this dead reckoning; curiously, many military men cannot, perhaps because the soldiers they drill are all too real to them.

The best reason to oppose the military-industrial complex is the most intimate: because it can kill your son or brother or cousin, and its social and economic fallout can destroy your town. But arguments from personal experience are consistently belittled. For instance, the only legitimate defense against a charge of prejudice is the oft-lampooned "some of my best friends are . . ." Yet this is inadmissible; the prescribed defense is to mist one's eyes, make a windy speech in which Martin Luther King Jr. is quoted copiously, and then go home and underpay your Guatemalan housekeeper.

There was a gem of a pop song in the late 1960s that defined the difference between Us and Them with stark clarity. Jimmy Webb wrote it; the title was "Galveston," and unlike most antiwar songs, which are full of high-minded claptrap about peace and universal brotherhood—empty platitudes by and for coked-up zombies—"Galveston" imagined a boy whose government had sent him far from home, God knows why, to kill or be killed by strangers, and this boy's only desire was to run once more with his girl on the beach of his hometown.

In the quadrennial assessment of the Men in Grey who wish to live in the White House, I ask a simple question: Will he (never yet a she) allow that eighteen-year-old boy in Galveston to walk the beach, freely, with his girl? Or will he strip this boy of his liberty, even his beer and cigarettes, and send him far from home, steal him from Galveston and steal Galveston from him—indeed, efface Galveston, so that all that remains is a name on a map, and all that made Galveston Galveston is gone gone gone.

During the Cold War our presidents became masters of spangled orotundity, of ghosted magniloquence, as the rotting carcasses piled up offstage. How could we possibly have endured three consecutive rulers such as JFK, LBJ, and RMN—deranged monograms who, their publicists assured us, dreamed Great Dreams. (The only compliment more glowing is that a president "made America believe in itself again," as Ronald of Bel Air was said to have done. Indeed, who among us will ever forget where she was at the moment she learned that Grenada had been liberated?)

Yes, these men thought big. Kennedy, after declaring that he and his Harvard touch-football-playing suckups were willing to make Middle America pay any price and bear any burden to perform the constitution-ally mandated task of preserving the libertarian democracies of Quemoy and Matsu, next set his sights on the moon, which had never done us any harm. (Presumably our Pulitzer Prize–winning historian had heard colorable tales of sluttish seleno-starlets just dying for one of those fabled forty-five-second Kennedy love marathons.) Johnson declared war on poverty, which he apparently intended to win by killing as many poor boys as possible in Vietnam. Then came Nixon. I suppose I am softer on Dick than the others because of his goofily awkward kindness toward his assistant and my dear lost friend, Carlos Narvaez. When Carlos would meet with the disgraced ex-president to go over the transcripts of those tapes, those sticky damned tapes, Nixon would ask, "Er, Carlos, can we get you anything: coffee, tea, . . . drugs?"

So there was a person, if not integrity, under the integument.

In one of those sententious post-Watergate books that were intended to burnish his reputation and make us forget about what Gene McCarthy called his fascistic misuse of the FBI and IRS (or is any use of the internal security system by definition a misuse?), Nixon quoted De Gaulle that "France was never true to herself unless she was engaged in a great enterprise." To which the Trickster added, "I have always believed that this was true of the United States as well. Defending and promoting peace and freedom around the world is a great enterprise. Only by rededicating ourselves to that goal will we remain true to ourselves."

True to ourselves. You might think you can be true to yourself by raising a family, planting a garden, participating in the life of a small and vital community, writing books about your people's history, building houses or farming land or simply studying with the birds, flowers, trees, God, and yourself, as Dvorak put it—but you would be wrong. Worse, you would be small, meager, mean, niggardly. The measure of a man's greatness is his willingness to abandon his family and go abroad to murder strangers on behalf of . . . your guess is as good as mine. Mr. Nixon's "great enterprises," I guess.

My daughter's lemonade stand is a great enterprise; the cabinetmaker's shop is a great enterprise; the town historical society's new museum is a great enterprise; the undertakings of the warped and scrofulous men who rule us call to mind Thoreau's remark on the pyramids:

"There is nothing to wonder at in them so much as the fact that so many men could be found degraded enough to spend their lives constructing a tomb for some ambitious booby, whom it would have been wiser and manlier to have drowned in the Nile."

We might better dispose of our own ambitious boobies in the River Nil. For they have their own pyramid: the American Empire, whose gift to thirtieth-century archeologists will not be Tutankhamenian baubles but rather Jerry Bruckheimer DVDs.

What, exactly, is in all this for us? What has *ever* been it in for us? "Malign neglect," we might say, Moynihan-like. For empire focuses our attention on matters distant and remote, affairs to which we are mere spectators. You can care about your backyard *or* Baghdad; you can't tend to both.

Alas, government has the power to forcibly remove an American from his backyard and send him to Baghdad. The essential rootlessness of the men who wield this power enables them, like General Grant, to do crimson calculus. (Roscoe Conkling poetized Grant's placelessness at the 1880 Republican convention: "When asked what state he hails from/ Our sole reply shall be—/ 'He hails from Appomattox/ With its famous apple tree.'")

Do you really think Henry Kissinger gave a damn how many Joe Doakses and LeRoy Washingtons he inscribed on the Vietnam Wall? He didn't know these men; he couldn't *imagine* them. They hadn't even the reality of a planchet on a Risk board.

The young men and women whose corpses are being shipped homeward on army cargo planes from the Middle East have no greater claim on the Bushian consience. He is, after all, as placeless as the others. Facile contemners of President Bush deride him as a "Texas cowboy." If only he were. Alas, President of the World Bush is a deracinated preppie, an Andover yell leader who blamed his first defeat for public office, in a 1978 congressional race, on "provincialism." It seems that the real cowboys were unimpressed by a petulant boarding-school cheerleader who was unable to pronounce correctly the name of the largest city in the district. (It was Lubbock, which is not exactly Sault Ste. Marie.)

Bush's helpmeet, Vice President Cheney of Haliburton, is so place-less that once he humbly determined himself to be the most qualified running mate Mr. Bush might have, he had to hop a plane to Wyoming and become an instant citizen of the Equality State so as to avoid violating the pettifogging constitutional clause that effectively prevents president and vice president from being residents of the same state. Bush and Cheney have no similar constitutional scruples when it comes to honoring Article 1, Section 8 of that forgotten document, which reserves to Congress the right to declare war, but then such hairsplitting is best left to epicene liberals.

So what to do?

My solution is no more "practical" than a Dorothy Day prayer or a Henry Thoreau spade. It is this: No statesman's coercive power should ever extend over people he does not know. If Bush and Hillary, Lieberman and Rumsfeld, and the Democracy Geeks of M Street want to pull their brats out of Sidwell and ship them overseas to kill whatever dusky primitives are our enemy of the week, so be it, but they have no claim upon my kin or my neighbors (or yours).

We are useful to them only as far as we follow orders, do not make trouble, and die on cue. The literary critic Paul Fussell, whose back and right thigh were ripped by shrapnel from a German shell in March 1945, explained, "It wasn't long before I could articulate for myself the message that war was sending the infantry soldier: 'You are expendable. Don't imagine that your family's good opinion of you will cut any ice here. You are just another body to be used. Since all can't be damaged or destroyed as they are fed into the machinery, some may survive, but that's not my fault. Most must be chewed up, and you'll probably be one of them. This is regrettable, but nothing can be done about it.'"

Well, one thing can be done about it. Don't go. Be a Carolyn Chute. Stay with your family. Your tribe. Your neighborhood. Your town. As Joe

Strummer of The Clash hummed, "It's up to you not to heed the call-up." Don't feed the war machine. You are not expendable, in your family's eyes or in God's. The soft young men in three-piece suits who write their little pamphlets proving that whatever slaughter our government is currently engaged in is a "just war" should be laughed back to the seminaries they quit. Thou shalt not kill means us, too.

I know, I know—it isn't gonna be that way.

I would like to blame television for making us a nation of cretins, lobotomized by that wasteland so vast it makes Newton Minnow look like a veritable Moby Dick of oracles. Is a resistance, a revival of small-scale politics possible when Mississippians prefer *The West Wing* to Welty? Ah, but physician, lacerate thyself: I sit listening to Neil Young's album *Greendale*, about a small-town family shattered (but also ennobled) by its fight against the modern world. About five minutes after ole' Neil shouts "It ain't an honor to be on TV—and it ain't a duty either," I get a phone call asking me to appear on a Rochester TV news show to discuss my late friend Barber Conable. I do it. Sorry Neil. Sorry Barber. It's TV, y'know?

And on that tube, or at least on the big screen that was both shrunk and supplanted by the tube, we can find clues pointing the way back. However much I might wish to secede from popular culture, I can't; it's the air I grew up breathing. It also, at its infrequent best, shows us the alternative America, the very real America excluded from The History Channel and the collected plagiarisms of Doris Kearns Goodwin.

Let us take 1940, and consider both the president of these United States and our most popular filmmaker. Like millions of Americans, Frank Capra loathed Franklin D. Roosevelt. Capra and FDR really were antitheses: the Sicilian boy dressed in rags who sold papers to put himself through Caltech and the lazy child of the patriciate, mocked by his arch cousin Alice as "Nancy"; the artist who saw his creation (Longfellow Deeds) as "the living symbol of the deep rebellion in every human heart—a growing resentment against being compartmentalized," and the prevaricating politician whose sympathies were always with the raw steel-toed-boot-to-the-head power of the state. Capra loved and respected women, coaxing outstanding performances from shy actresses Jean Arthur and Donna Reed; FDR married his shy cousin—and then cheated on her.

The gap between rulers and ruled can be measured in a thousand anecdotal ways. My maternal great-grandmother, an immigrant from Northern Italy, cursed FDR for blackening the final years of her life. Two of her sons were conscripted into Mr. Roosevelt's Army, and though she well understood that Hitler was evil, Mussolini was a nasty fascist, and Tojo had bombed Pearl Harbor, she was unwilling to watch the boys she bore and raised die in the Pacific in an international quarrel to which she was not a party. Or as a great Kentucky pugilist once put it, "I ain't got no quarrel with no Viet Cong."

Do you call this selfish? Were Paulina Stella and Muhammad Ali pinched and ungenerous? Certainly the chickenhawks who want the U.S. to remake the world would say so, though as a *Saturday Evening Post* editorialist once put it, "Very few of those who maintain that it is sweet to die for one's country have ever done it."

In any war the dissenter is maligned (Millard Fillmore, 1864), mocked (Henry Adams, 1898), jailed (Eugene V. Debs, 1918), calumnied (Charles Lindbergh, 1941), shot (Martin Luther King Jr., 1968), or slandered as treasonous (take a look around). The mother or wife or lover who wishes to keep the soldier home is "selfish"; the patriot who decries the martial tattoo of the drums is "unpatriotic." I suppose in this light Paulina was just another comely young garlic-eater whose looks had gone to her waistline; just another vote in the mob, just another Social Security number, just another "brood so[w], having sons to be put into the army and made into fertilizer," as socialist hellraiser Kate Richards O'Hare said of the women of World War I America—a crack for which she was arrested under Woodrow Wilson's Espionage Act and thrown into jail.

Paulina's fellow Italian immigrant Frank Capra insisted, in his charmingly bitter autobiography, *The Name Above the Title*, that "[w]hen I see a crowd, I see a collection of free individuals: each a unique person; each a king or a queen; each a story that would fill a book; each an island of human dignity." But Capra was a sentimental old fool who was guilty of the "reactionary idealization of small-town America," according to his sneering biographer Joseph McBride.

(It's bad enough being dead, but to get stuck with a dimwitted biographer: oh, the horror. McBride is disgusted that Capra "never progressed beyond a superficial understanding of Marxism. His deep-seated emotional bias against collectivism and in favor of rugged individualism kept him from a proper appreciation of the New Deal." Indeed, Capra voted against FDR four times.)

Like Frank Capra, the best radicals are reactionaries at heart. They despise the official order, be it state capitalism, militarism, communism, or what have you, but wish not merely to remove the malignancy but to replace it with an organic system, rooted in human nature and human affection. However angry, theirs—ours—is a politics of love.

They are not mere rebels without a cause. Instead, they value the importance of "doin' your own thing in your own time," as those two deeply American filmmakers Dennis Hopper and Peter Fonda (our Kansas-Nebraska Act-ors) said in their druggy paean to the pioneer virtues, *Easy Rider*.

I don't really have to convince you that *Easy Rider* is a reactionary picture, do I? The only characters depicted as unqualifiably virtuous are the homesteading family, living on their own acreage, raising their own food, teaching their young. If they're not Treichlers then Dennis Hopper is playing Ron Ziegler. The only American Dream worth the snores is based in liberty and a community- (or family-) oriented independence, which the filmmakers associate with the country's founders. Dennis Hopper (an admittedly unorthodox Kansas Republican) and Peter Fonda (a gun-loving libertarian) did not make a movie glorifying tripping hippies and condemning the southern gun culture; rather, as an exasperated Fonda explained, "My movie is about the *lack* of freedom. My heroes are not right, they're wrong. . . . Liberty's become a whore, and we're all taking the easy ride."

I go on about what I am sure is now a ludicrously unfashionable movie because *Easy Rider* was groping toward a truth that might have set Americans free. The hippies and the small-town southerners gathered in the diner; the small farmers and shaggy communards: they were *on the same side*. The side of liberty, of locally based community, of independence from the war machine, the welfare state, the bureaucratic prison whose wardens were McNamara, Rockefeller, Bundy, and the wise men and wealthy men who had never grasped Paul Goodman's point—or perhaps they had grasped it all too well, and wrestled it into submission—that "[i]t is only the anarchists who are really conservative, for they want to conserve sun and space, animal nature, primary community, experimenting inquiry."

It is only the anarchists who are really conservative.

Is the CSA, the most hopeful development in the recent history of American agriculture, conservative, anarchist, radical, reactionary, or all, blessedly all, of the above? I speak not of the Confederate States of America, that Lost Cause fatally flawed at conception, but community-supported agriculture, whereby Americans buy fresh, organically grown fruits and vegetables directly from the farmer. Elba, New York, I am proud to say, is home to the 500-acre Porter Farms, one of the nation's model CSAs. Steve Porter, the hockey player who was its guiding spirit, died in June 2004, just after his daughter Katie was graduated as valedictorian of the Elba High Class of '04 but too soon to see his daughter Sarah give the valediction for the Class of '05.

My friend Bart Dentino and I would see Steve at the farm every Saturday morn. Dying of brain cancer, glassy-eyed, robbed of equilibrium, looking like hell, he would mumble stoically, by way of heroically insufficient explanation, about "allergies" when I stupidly asked him how he was doing. How was he doing? He was dying. Yet he was giving life, too; like Wendell Berry, Steve was showing us what an economy based on the human scale, on stewardship of the earth, on production for local consumption, and, yes, on free enterprise and mutualism, might look like. Steve was showing us the alternative American future.

You will say that mine is an idle and impossible dream; I will reply that 340,000 Americans participate in community-supported agriculture, and the number grows annually. I will reply that the number of homeschoolers has grown from a handful of spirited truants in 1960 to 1.5 million today. I will reply that the number of American households without a television set is rising—and that the lack of this amenity of enmity is utterly unrelated to the incidence of poverty. I will reply that the percentage of Americans who refuse to implicate themselves in choiceless elections of the Gush-Bore and Kerry-Bush variety has risen with such a steely inexorability over the last couple of decades that frantic political scientists are proposing every method of increasing voter turnout—shifting historic election days, penalizing nonvoters, paying voters—save one: giving voters a real choice.

I am not about to hold myself up as an example of Life Properly Lived. Hell, everything I grow with my brown thumb withers on the vine. But we do a couple of things right. For instance, in our home we celebrate the arrival of months and seasons with literature and food—preferably both. (Which is why I crave November.)

Some months are feasts, others are famine.

On the summer solstice, I read to Gretel from Ray Bradbury's *Dandelion Wine*, with its beautiful evocation of the first day of summer. As a girl, my grandmother picked dandelions that were transubstantiated into wine in her parents' speakeasy in the western New York hamlet of Lime Rock. Every couple of years Lucine, Gretel, and I pull out the family recipe and get to work picking the gorgeous yellow flowers (they are not weeds!) for our own batch of the nectar. I suppose this violates some child-labor statute or other, but as in Bradbury's novel, the bottles of wine may be uncorked over the years to bring back sweet memories. (And I tell you, sometimes the lessons take. A while back, we were trying to decide whence to order our evening's pizza: Andy's, which is run by the father of one of Gretel's classmates, or Santino's, which then had stores in Elba and adjacent Oakfield. "Let's get Andy's," Gretel declared. "Santino's is a chain." *That's* my girl!)

When July ripens the berries on the vines that overspread our yard, we share biscuits and baseball stories. Casey can strike out all he wants to; blackberry-raspberry shortcake is always a hit.

August, on the other sweaty palm, has inspired fewer poets than any of its eleven sisters. William D. Gallagher, the Ohio poet of the 1840s, composed an ode titled "August" but couldn't do much better than "Tediously pass the hours/ And vegetation wilts, with blister'd root." We eschew the wilted greens in the garden in favor of juicy tomatoes underneath melted mozzarella.

But August yields to September, and one of my favorite rituals: the expectant drive past the Roanoke Apple Farm, waiting for the magic word "Cider" to appear on the message board. October is Poe and Hawthorne and pumpkins that have been cooked, pureed, and otherwise rendered delicious.

I love November, from which William Cullen Bryant begged "one smile more, distant departing sun." At mid-month, Lucine bakes a carrot-pineapple cake that is the gustatory highlight of my birthday. A week later, my grandmother, who picked dandelions for wine so many springs ago, will hand-crank the stale bread that becomes the dressing on our Thanksgiving table. She greets my father's jab, "Pepperidge Farm?" with a glare cold enough to freeze Miles Standish. Like our Pilgrim forbears, we are grateful for many things in November—and the blessings of family most of all.

December is all cookies and sentiment: Truman Capote's "A Christmas Memory," Mary Wilkins Freeman's "Christmas Jenny," and of course Clement Moore's poem are inspiring caloric accompaniments.

At Christmastide, which post-Americans would like to rename "the holidays" (and isn't the root of that word the most un-secular "holy day"?),

I torture one and all with "Jingle Bells" and Christina Rosetti, but the loveliest moment of the season occurs at 7:00 p.m. on Christmas Eve, when much of Elba gathers within a barn on the Yunker farm out on Transit Road.

We shuffle in, seasonally cheerful if usually cold, for the barn is unheated. The cattle are lowing. A calf or two, reliably balky, keep watch over a crib. The children put on their kaftans, the shepherds take staffs, the angels don haloes, Mary cradles a baby doll. Gretel has played the Virgin Mother more than once; she wants to be an actress, and what part can surpass her role on this night? They sit and stand in silence, in a reverence not even broken when the calf kicks up some hay.

The service lasts perhaps half an hour, not long enough for frostbite to set in. We sing "Joy to the World," "O Little Town of Bethlehem," "Away in a Manger," "The First Noel," and "It Came Upon a Midnight Clear," punctuated by readings from Isaiah and Luke. The Presbyterian minister offers a thought much too brief and apt to be called a sermon.

The barn goes dark, lit only by a single candle. We sing "Silent Night" in the darkness. Sleep in heavenly peace. We leave the barn in a fellowship that is at once deeply particularistic, bound by place, yet also as universal as Christ's love. They'll know we are Christians, as the hymn goes.

Heavenly peace. The Little Way. The Way of Love. What do you say?

Bibliographical Note

Footnotes hobble essays, and since I wanted this book to have an essayistic quality, I have shooed them away. Where felicity has permitted, I have cited sources within the text. The others are listed hereunder.

INTRODUCTION

Material quoted herein is from Allen Tate, *Essays of Four Decades* (Wilmington, DE, 1999); Walter Block and Llewellyn H. Rockwell Jr., *Man, Economy, and Liberty: Essays in Honor of Murray N. Rothbard* (Auburn, AL, 1988); Robert Frost, *Complete Poems of Robert Frost* (New York, 1967); and Vachel Lindsay, *Collected Poems* (New York, 1925).

CHAPTER ONE

Dominic Sandbrook's *Eugene McCarthy: The Rise and Fall of Postwar American Liberalism* (New York, 2004) is snide but informative, especially on McCarthy's prepolitical years. I have also quoted from McCarthy's *Up 'Til Now: A Memoir* (New York, 1987); *Limits of Power* (New York, 1967); *The Ultimate Tyranny* (New York, 1980); and *Ground Fog and Night* (New York, 1979); as well as Eugene McCarthy (Keith C. Burris, ed.), *No-Fault Politics: Modern Presidents, the Press, and Reformers* (New York, 1998); James David Barber, *Presidential Character: Predicting Performance in the White House* (Englewood Cliffs, NJ, 1972); Richard N. Goodwin, *Remembering America: A Voice from the Sixties* (Boston, 1988); Ronald Steel, *In Love with Night: The American Romance with Robert Kennedy* (New York, 2000); Jim Castelli, "McCarthy Challenges the System," *Nation*, August 30, 1975; "A Mighty Long Fall: An Interview with Eugene McCarthy," *Chronicles*,

July 1996; and Paul Likoudis, "Eugene McCarthy: Still Right After All These Years," *Wanderer*, December 2, 2004.

Godfrey Hodgson, *The Gentleman from New York: Daniel Patrick Moynihan* (Boston, 2000) and Douglas Schoen, *Pat: A Biography of Daniel Patrick Moynihan* (New York, 1979) are the extant Moynihan biographies. There will be others. The festschrift *Daniel Patrick Moynihan: The Intellectual in Public Life* (Baltimore, 1998) contains several illuminating essays, among them James Q. Wilson's delightful "Pat," which includes a memorable description of the unathletic Moynihan conscripted into a Harvard faculty softball game. For my money, Moynihan's best book of essays is *Coping: On the Practice of Government* (New York, 1975), which features his 1961 profile of New York Democrats, "'Bosses' and 'Reformers.'" I have also used Moynihan's *Counting Our Blessings: Reflections on the Future of America* (Boston, 1980); Robert A. Slayton, *Empire Statesman: The Rise and Redemption of Al Smith* (New York, 2001); Henry Adams, *The Education of Henry Adams* (New York, 1931 [1918]); Robert A. Caro, *The Power Broker: Robert Moses and the Fall of New York* (New York, 1974); Henry Cabot Lodge, *Daniel Webster* (Boston, 1886); Charles H. Hamilton, ed., *Fugitive Essays: Selected Writings of Frank Chodorov* (Indianapolis, 1980); Daniel Patrick Moynihan, "Do We Still Need the C.I.A.?" *New York Times*, May 19, 1991; Moynihan's "Reflections at Fifteen: New York State and the Federal Fisc: XV" (1991); Todd S. Purdum, "The Newest Moynihan," *New York Times Magazine*, August 7, 1994; Jonathan Alter, "The Brain and the Pig Trough," *Newsweek*, February 15, 1993; Jacob Heilbrun, "The Moynihan Enigma," *American Prospect*, July-August 1997; Jacob Weisberg, "For the Sake of Argument," *New York Times Magazine*, November 5, 2000; Thomas L. Friedman, "Lily-Livered Neo-Wilsonian! The New Political Tag Game," *New York Times*, October 25, 1992; Bill Kauffman, "Big City in Little Pieces," *American Enterprise*, June 2002; "Live with Daniel Patrick Moynihan," *American Enterprise*, June 2002; and Benjamin Smith, "A Debate Grows in Brooklyn," *New York Sun*, May 8, 2002.

CHAPTER TWO

Most of the material in this chapter came from past issues of the *Catholic Worker*, which I have tried to cite in the text. Day's *The Long Loneliness* (New York, 1959) and Robert Coles's *Dorothy Day: A Radical Devotion* (Boston, 1987) are essential. I have also quoted from John Lukacs, *Confessions of an Original Sinner* (New York, 1990); Garry Wills, *Confessions of a Conservative* (New York, 1979); Dwight Macdonald, *Memoirs of a Revolutionist* (New York, 1957); John Tyee Fain and Thomas Daniel Young, eds., *The Literary Correspondence of Donald Davidson and Allen Tate* (Athens, GA, 1974); David W. Southern, *John LaFarge and the Limits of Catholic Interracialism* (Baton Rouge, LA, 1996); Peter McDonough, *Men Astutely Trained: A History of the Jesuits in the American Century* (New York, 1992); Nancy L. Roberts, *Dorothy Day and the Catholic Worker* (Albany, NY, 1984); Gregory P. Pavlik, ed., *Forgotten Lessons: Selected Essays of John T. Flynn* (Irvington-on-Hudson, NY, 1995); James O'Gara, ed., *Catholicism in America* (New York, 1954); Patrick G. Coy, ed., *A Revolution of the Heart: Essays on the Catholic Worker* (Philadelphia, 1988); William J. Thorn, Phillip M. Runkel, and Susan Mountin, *Dorothy Day and the Catholic Worker Movement: Centenary Essays* (Milwaukee, 2001); Patricia O'Toole, *The Five of Hearts: An Intimate Portrait of Henry Adams and His Friends, 1880–1918* (New York, 1990); Arthur M. Schlesinger Jr., *The Vital Center: The Politics of Freedom* (Boston, 1949); Robert Ellsberg, ed., *By Little and Little: The Selected Writings of Dorothy Day* (New York, 1983); Dorothy Day, *On Pilgrimage: The Sixties* (New York, 1972); *I'll Take My Stand: The South and the Agrarian Tradition* (Baton Rouge, LA, 1977 [1930]), by "Twelve Southerners"; William F. Buckley Jr., "The Catholic in the Modern World: A Conservative View," *Commonweal*, December 16, 1960; J. P. Chamberlain, "Looking Backward: Ten Years of *Free America*," *Free America*, Winter 1946–47; Herbert Agar, "The Task for Conservatism," *American Review*, April 1934; Allen Tate, "Notes on Liberty and Property," *American Review*, 1936; Donald Davidson, "Agrarianism for Commuters," *American*

Review, 1933; Karl Hess, "An Open Letter to Barry Goldwater," *Ramparts*, August 1969; Henry Clay Evans Jr., "Liberty Under the Old Order," *American Review*, 1936; Anthony Novitsky, "Peter Maurin's Green Revolution: The Radical Implications of Reactionary Social Catholicism," *Review of Politics*, January 1975; David J. O'Brien, "American Social Thought in the 1930s," Ph.D. diss., University of Rochester, 1965; Murray N. Rothbard, "The Transformation of the American Right," *Continuum*, Summer 1964; Patricia McNeal, "Origins of the Catholic Peace Movement," *Review of Politics*, July 1973; Anthony T. Bouscaren, "The Catholic Peaceniks," *National Review*, March 8, 1966; and Edward S. Shapiro, "Catholic Agrarian Thought and the New Deal," *Catholic Historical Review*, 1979.

CHAPTER THREE

Grant Wood's "Revolt Against the City," which deserves a handsome reprint, may be found in James Dennis, *Grant Wood: A Study in American Art and Culture* (Columbia, MO, 1986). E. Bradford Burns's *Kinship with the Land: Regionalist Thought in Iowa, 1894–1942* (Iowa City, IA, 1996) is an absolute gem. For more on Sinclair Lewis as a regionalist, see my *America First! Its History, Culture, and Politics* (Amherst, NY, 1995). I have also relied on Joseph S. Czestochowski, *John Steuart Curry and Grant Wood: A Portrait of Rural America* (Columbia, MO, 1981); University of Kansas Museum of Art, *John Steuart Curry* (Lawrence, KS, 1970); Laurence E. Schmeickebier, *John Steuart Curry's Pageant of America* (New York, 1943); Darrell Garwood, *Artist in Iowa* (New York, 1944); Hazel E. Brown, *Grant Wood and Marvin Cone: Artists of an Era* (Ames, IA, 1987 [1972]); Jan Swafford, *Charles Ives: A Life with Music* (New York, 1996); Jay Fultz, *In Search of Donna Reed* (Iowa City, IA, 1998); Robert L. Dorman, *Revolt of the Provinces: The Regionalist Movement in America, 1920–1945* (Chapel Hill, NC, 1993); Timothy Murphy, *The Deed of Gift* (Ashland, OR, 1998); Paul Engle, *American Song* (Garden City, NY, 1934); John C. Skipper,

Meredith Willson: The Unsinkable Music Man (El Dorado Hills, CA, 2003); Helen Ristau, *Meredith Willson: River City's Music Man* (Mason City, IA, 2001); Robert Gard, *Grassroots Theater: A Search for Regional Arts in America* (Madison, WI, 1999 [1955]); Mildred J. Loomis, *Alternative Americas: An Informal History by the "Grandmother of the Counter-Culture"* (New York, 1982); Steven Watson, *The Harlem Renaissance: Hub of African-American Culture, 1920–1930* (New York, 1995); Rufus W. Griswold, ed., *The Poets and Poetry of America* (Philadelphia, 1858); Wayne S. Cole, *America First: The Battle Against Intervention, 1940–1941* (Madison, WI, 1953); Clarence E. Pickett, *For More Than Bread* (Boston, 1953); Jay G. Sigmund, *The Ridge Road: Short Stories and Poems* (Cedar Rapids, IA, 1930); Ralph Borsodi, *Flight from the City* (New York, 1933); W. P. Kinsella, *The Iowa Baseball Confederacy* (Boston, 1986); Stefan Fatsis, *Wild and Outside: How a Renegade Minor League Revived the Spirit of Baseball in America's Heartland* (New York, 1995); William Appleman Williams, *Some Presidents: From Wilson to Nixon* (New York, 1972); Ruth Sarles, *A Story of America First: The Men and Women Who Opposed U.S. Intervention in World War II* (Westport, CT, 2003); Paul Engle, *Corn* (New York, 1939); Ed Ferreter, "Jay G. Sigmund and Grant Wood," *Books at Iowa*, April 1985; Todd Kimm, "What's a Rebel Editor to Do?" *Iowa City Icon*, December 7, 2000; Bill Kauffman, "Subsidies to the Arts: Cultivating Mediocrity," Cato Institute, August 8, 1990; Bill Kauffman, "Culture in Inner America," *American Enterprise*, July-August 2004; and Bill Kauffman, "Allegania the Beautiful," *American Enterprise*, July 1998.

CHAPTER FOUR

The Wendell Berry books from which I have quoted are *A Place on Earth* (San Francisco, 1983); *Watch With Me* (New York, 1994); *Hannah Coulter* (Washington, DC, 2004); *That Distant Land* (Washington, DC, 2004); *Collected Poems: 1957–1982* (San Francisco, 1985); *The Wild Birds* (San Francisco, 1986); *Fidelity* (New York, 1992); *The Long-Legged House*

(Washington, DC, 2004 [1969]); *A Continuous Harmony* (New York, 1972); *The Hidden Wound* (New York, 1970); *Citizenship Papers* (Washington, DC, 2003); and *Home Economics* (San Francisco, 1987). I have also used Steven Stoll, *Larding the Lean Earth: Soil and Society in Nineteenth-Century America* (New York, 2002); Jay P. Corrin, *G. K. Chesterton and Hilaire Belloc: The Battle Against Modernity* (Athens, OH, 1978); Paul Goodman, *New Reformation: Notes of a Neolithic Conservative* (New York, 1970); Richard Hofstadter, *The American Political Tradition* (New York, 1973 [1948]); Vernon Parrington, *Main Currents in American Thought* (New York, 1930); John W. Jeffries, *Wartime America: The World War II Home Front* (Chicago, 1996); John P. Marquand, *So Little Time* (Boston, 1943); Edward Dumbauld, ed., *The Political Writings of Thomas Jefferson* (Indianapolis, 1955); William Stafford, *Every War Has Two Losers* (Minneapolis, 2003); C. Vann Woodward, *Tom Watson: Agrarian Rebel* (New York, 1972 [1938]); Edgar Lee Masters, *Spoon River Anthology* (New York, 1916); Edward S. Shapiro, "Decentralist Intellectuals and the New Deal," *Journal of American History*, March 1972; Gordon L. Iseminger, "North Dakota's Cornhusking Contests, 1939–1941," *Agricultural History*, Winter 1997; Roy L. Brooks, "What About Souter's Human Resume?" *New York Times*, August 1, 1990; and Wayne S. Cole, "America First and the South, 1940–1941," *Journal of Southern History*, February 1956.

CHAPTER FIVE

I have quoted from Carolyn Chute's *The Beans of Egypt, Maine* (New York, 1985); *Merry Men* (New York, 1994); and *Snow Man* (New York, 1999); as well as numerous letters Carolyn has written me over the years. I have also used Karl Hess, *Mostly on the Edge: An Autobiography* (Amherst, NY, 1999); Robert Scheer, ed., *Eldridge Cleaver: Post-Prison Writings and Speeches* (New York, 1969); Christopher Lasch, *The True and Only Heaven: Progress and Its Critics* (New York, 1991); Christopher Lasch (Elisabeth Lasch-Quinn, ed.), *Women and the Common Life: Love, Marriage, and Feminism* (New

York, 1997); Edith Wharton, *Ghosts* (New York, 1937); John Steinbeck, *The Grapes of Wrath* (New York, 1939); Nick Salvatore, *Eugene V. Debs: Citizen and Socialist* (Urbana, IL, 1982); H. L. Mencken, *A Carnival of Buncombe: Writings on Politics* (Chicago, 1984 [1956]); Mother Jones, *Autobiography of Mother Jones* (Chicago, 1925); Philip Foner, ed., *Mother Jones Speaks: Collected Writings and Speeches* (New York, 1983); Dale Featherling, *Mother Jones: The Miners' Angel* (Carbondale, IL, 1974); Edward Steel, ed., *The Speeches and Writings of Mother Jones* (Pittsburgh, 1988); W. A. Swanberg, *Norman Thomas: The Last Idealist* (New York, 1976); Richard E. Welch Jr., *The Presidencies of Grover Cleveland* (Lawrence, KS, 1988); Robert Nisbet, *The Quest for Community: A Study in the Ethics of Order and Freedom* (San Francisco, 1990 [1953]); Christopher Lasch, "The Obsolescence of Left and Right," *New Oxford Review*, April 1989; Ian Young, "Paul Goodman: American Anarchist," *Reason*, June 1974; Bill Kauffman, "A Tennessee Political Ramble," *American Enterprise*, March-April 1998; Bill Kauffman, "The Militia of Love," *Chronicles*, November 1999; Karl Hess, "An Open Letter to Barry Goldwater," *Ramparts*, August 1969; Karl Hess, "Living in Freedom," *Reason*, May 1978; Murray Kempton, "Goldwater Finds His Sorenson," *New Republic*, August 8, 1964; James Boyd, "From Far Right to Far Left—and Farther—with Karl Hess," *New York Times Magazine*, December 6, 1970; and "Interview with Eldridge Cleaver," *Reason*, February 1986.

CHAPTER SIX

I have quoted from Robert J. Rayback, *Millard Fillmore: Biography of a President* (Buffalo, NY, 1959); Michael F. Holt, *The Rise and Fall of the American Whig Party* (New York, 1999); John Jay Chapman, *William Lloyd Garrison* (New York, 1913); Frank H. Severance, ed., *Millard Fillmore Papers* (Buffalo, NY, 1907); Henry Mayer, *All on Fire: William Lloyd Garrison and the Abolition of Slavery* (New York, 1998); John Gardner, *The Sunlight Dialogues* (New York, 1972); Andrew W. Young, *History of the Town of War-*

saw (Buffalo, NY, 1869); Lewis Perry, *Radical Abolitionism: Anarchy and the Government of God in Antislavery Thought* (Knoxville, TN, 1995 [1973]); Gerrit Smith, *The True Office of Civil Government* (New York, 1851); *Speeches of Gerrit Smith in Congress* (New York, 1855); Ralph Volney Harlow, *Gerrit Smith: Philanthropist and Reformer* (New York, 1939); Edgar Lee Masters, *Lincoln, The Man* (New York, 1931); Ross Lockridge, *Raintree County* (Boston, 1948); Dumas Malone, *The Sage of Monticello* (Boston, 1981); Frank L. Klement, *Limits of Dissent: Clement L. Vallandigham and the Civil War* (Lexington, KY, 1970); James L. Vallandigham, *Life of Clement L. Vallandigham* (Baltimore, 1872); John Greenleaf Whittier, *Complete Poetical Works of John Greenleaf Whittier* (Boston, 1882); Elbert J. Benton, *The Movement for Peace Without a Victory During the Civil War* (Cleveland, OH, 1918); Claude G. Bowers, *The Tragic Era: The Revolution after Lincoln* (Cambridge, MA, 1929); Margaret Mitchell, *Gone with the Wind* (New York, 1936); Stephen Vincent Benet, *Burning City* (New York, 1936); Lewis Bishop, "Seth M. Gates," Warsaw, NY, 1963; "A Notable Landmark," *Historical Wyoming*, July 1951; "Origins of the Abolitionist Movement," *Historical Wyoming*, October 1959; Neil Johnson, "Sanford E. Church: Arguably Albion's Most Prominent Citizen," *Albion Advertiser*, August 1, 2003; Bill Kauffman, "The Civil War Returns," *American Enterprise*, March 2003; "Live with Shelby Foote," *American Enterprise*, January-February 2001; and Sanford E. Church, "The Revolutionary Designs of the Abolitionists," printed speech, October 13, 1863.

Conclusion

I have quoted from Jay Parini, *Robert Frost: A Life* (New York, 1999); Paul Fussell, *Wartime: Understanding and Behavior in the Second World War* (New York, 1989); Frank Capra, *The Name Above the Title* (New York, 1971); Joseph McBride, *Frank Capra: The Catastrophe of Success* (New York, 1992); Nancy Hardin and Marilyn Schlossberg, eds., *Easy Rider* (New York, 1969); Thomas Graham Belden and Marva Robins Belden, *So Fell the*

Angels (Boston, 1956); Henry David Thoreau, *Walden and "Civil Disobedience,"* (New York, 1960 [1854]; Taylor Stoehr, ed., *Drawing the Line: The Political Essays of Paul Goodman* (New York, 1977); Bill Minutaglio, *First Son: George W. Bush and the Bush Family Dynasty* (New York, 1999); Walter Karp, *Politics of War* (New York, 1980); William Cullen Bryant, *Poetical Works of William Cullen Bryant* (New York, 1887); Richard Nixon, *In the Arena: A Memoir of Victory, Defeat, and Renewal* (New York, 1990); and Robert Hilburn, "Rockers Rally 'Round the Flag," *Los Angeles Times*, June 30, 1985.

Index

About the Author

BILL KAUFFMAN is the author of five books, including the localist manifesto *Dispatches from the Muckdog Gazette*, which won the 2003 national "Sense of Place" award from Writers & Books. His other books include a novel, a travel book, and works about American isolationists and critics of progress. He writes for the *Wall Street Journal*, the *American Enterprise*, *Counterpunch*, and the *American Conservative*, among other publications. Kauffman lives in his native Genesee County, New York, with his wife Lucine and their daughter Gretel.